# EVOLUTION
## The Universe, Life, Cultures, Ethnicity, Religion, Science and Technology

by

David E. Tivel

DORRANCE PUBLISHING CO., INC.
PITTSBURGH, PENNSYLVANIA 15222

Dorrance Publishing Co., Inc.
701 Smithfield Street
Pittsburgh, PA 15222
Visit our website at *www.dorrancebookstore.com*

ISBN: 978-1-4349-1816-1
eISBN: 978-1-4349-1736-2

# CONTENTS

# PREFACE

This is a book about the evolution of our universe, life on Earth, cultures, ethnicity, religion, science, and technology. Evolution is a gradual change, usually for the better. It is a process by which something changes over time into a different and usually more complex form. Our universe has evolved, life has evolved, cultures and ethnicity have evolved, religion has evolved, and science and technology have evolved. Everything has evolved. We as individuals evolve. Change is inevitable. Evolution is inevitable.

Many readers of this book may have deeply embedded beliefs that conflict with some of what is presented herein. I also had conflicts I needed to resolve. As a child, I attended Catholic schools where moral and ethical values as well as religious tenets were engrained. As a young adult, I graduated from a state university (San Diego State) having studied math, physics, and engineering. I continued my education by taking classes with the University of Maryland while serving in the U.S. Army, and upon completion of my service continued with graduate work at the American University in Washington, DC. My work was always in science and technology-related areas. However, all the while there were questions with respect to my education and my scientific knowledge that needed to be answered and for which I didn't have time to pursue during my working career. Realizing some of these questions were due to a lack of up-to-date knowledge and understanding, I needed to evolve. Some research time was needed. This book is an outgrowth of that research, which I thoroughly enjoyed, and a treatise on some of the information and ideas acquired with respect to the evolution of the universe, life, cultures, ethnicity, religion, science, and technology.

I am indebted to those listed in the References section, in addition to the contributors of hundreds of articles, presentations, blogs, etc., on the Internet from which ideas and material were gathered. Hopefully, you will find this book enlightening. We are very fortunate to live in such a wonderful world at this remarkable time in history.

David E. Tivel

# INTRODUCTION

The universe, life, cultures, ethnicity, religion, science, and technology are vast subjects for which extensive thought and research have been performed by many great minds over thousands of years. Our current state of existence has evolved to what it is today because of our curiosity, needs, and the environments in which we live. Rapidly evolving technologies have made it possible to delve deeper into understanding our universe, life, and the sciences, and yet all that we know is still infinitely less than all that remains unknown. Shared attitudes, values, goals, and practices that characterize group cultures and ethnicity have evolved over time and have become more complex over time. With respect to religions, thousands of denominations have evolved to further guide us in our attitudes, values, and goals. An almost endless number of books have been written on these subjects. Additionally, since the advent of the Internet, information on just about everything is available from home computers.

Since the beginning of mankind our curiosity and quest for knowledge has been unending. Astronomers, cosmologists, and other scientists have devoted their working lives toward a deeper understanding of the universe and its origin; anthropologists, archaeologists, and sociologists continue to research into the origin and evolution of human life, cultures, and ethnicity; biologists and botanists study various forms of life and have altered many of them, especially in the area of food sources; sociologists, theologians, and clergy expound deep thoughts on religion, providing frameworks by which various societies live their lives; and people from many disciplines perform research to satisfy our curiosities and needs leading to advancements in science and technology. There is a continuum of change which can be recognized in just about everything.

The universe, life, cultures, ethnicity, religion, science, and technology are inextricably intertwined and are forever changing, and in so doing they generally become more complex while optimistically providing for better lives. There are many interdependencies such that when a change in one occurs, it sparks change in something else. Such changes are not unidirectional. For example, environmental changes affect biologic changes and biologic changes in turn alter the environment. Life forms are dependent on their respective environments and environments are affected by the life forms that inhabit them. Biologists now recognize the evolution of species based on the work of Darwin and his successors, and science has led the way to evolving new enhanced species of plants and animals to better serve mankind.

Everything evolves over time. Just as things have evolved in the past, we can expect them to evolve in the future. The past provides the building blocks for the future. Because of our curiosity we are always looking for new information. Because of our changing needs and changing environments, we are constantly searching for new solutions and adapting to new situations. Modern humanity is just a snapshot in time. We have evolved from the past and will evolve into the future. Throughout this book an attempt is made at some predictions for the future—where evolutionary processes might take us.

**Hubble's Deepest View of the Universe—Galaxies Galore**

Retrieved from:
http://hubblesite.org/gallery/album/the_universe/pr2009031a/

Credit: NASA, ESA, G. Illingworth (UCO/Lick Observatory and the University of California, Santa Cruz), R. Bouwens (UCO/Lick Observatory and Leiden University), and the HUDF09 Team.

# CHAPTER 1

## Evolution: The Universe

We have often heard the phrase "from the beginning of time." Time as we know it started with the birth of our universe, referred to as the "Big Bang," 13.73±0.12 billion years ago (within 1% accuracy). More accurately, the Big Bang is now coined by cosmologist as the "Inflationary Hot Big Bang." And, we now learn from cosmologists that perhaps our universe may be one of many universes in an infinite cosmos. The cause of the Inflationary Hot Big Bang that initiated our universe is still undetermined, but theories abound and scientists seem to be getting closer to an explanation. Cosmologists have determined that our universe is, at a minimum, 93.2 billion light years across (46.6 billion light years distance from a central point or about 3.4 times greater than the distance of 13.7 billion light years that we can view with our most powerful telescopes). The maximum distance to which we could possibly see with the most sophisticated equipment is called the time horizon. The time horizon is the time since the Big Bang.

Evidence for the birth of our universe can be seen in the cosmic microwave background. Created in a annihilation of matter and antimatter seconds after the Big Bang, trapped in the hot plasma of the expanding universe for 380,000 years, and then suddenly released when the universe cooled to the point that elec-

1

trons and nuclei could combine into atoms allowing light to travel much more freely, the cosmic microwave background has been on an uninterrupted voyage through space for close to 13.7 billion years and is one of the most important clues about the history and nature of our universe. An extraordinary aspect of the cosmic microwave background is that it tells us our universe was ringing with sound during its first 380,000 years. These ripples were the seeds from which slightly overdense and slightly underdense regions in our universe formed. Overdense regions provided greater gravitation attraction, which in turn caused further accretion of matter. These ripples frozen in space at the instant of inflation formed the seeds from which galaxies and all later structure grew. George Smoot of the University of California, Berkeley, won half of the 2006 Nobel Prize in Physics for his role as leader of the team that used the COBE satellite to discover the temperature variations in the cosmic microwave background. Several timelines are included at the end of this chapter: Timeline for Our Universe, Timeline of Cosmological Theories and Discoveries, and Timeline of Artificial Satellites and Space Probes.

Our universe is expanding at an increasing rate, and in fact, per Einstein's general relativity, it is expanding at a rate faster than the speed of light. Some galaxies viewed today that were within the time horizon of 13.7 billion years ago have since moved outside of the time horizon. In the future, fewer and fewer galaxies will be visible as the universe expands and more and more galaxies move outside of the time horizon. If the laws of physics are the same outside of our observable universe as they are inside, we can conclude that our universe is at a minimum 39 times as large as the observable part (using the volume of a sphere to be $4/3\pi r3$ we get $4/3\pi46,600,000,000^3 / 4/3\pi13,730,000,000^3 = 39.1$). In fact, if inflation as we understand it is true, our universe could even be much larger than 39 times the observable part. In spite of its vast size and the increasing rate of expansion, our universe is still and will always be finite in size and time of existence; however, many cosmologists now believe that the cosmos (as opposed to our universe) is infinite in size and time. If that is true, the concept of a multiverse (i.e., many universes in the cosmos) seems very plausible. While the conditions that allowed for our universe occurred 13.73 billion years ago, it is quite possible such conditions could have occurred many times over an infinite timeframe in an infinite cosmos. Astronomers have found a pattern of concentric circles in four different areas of the cosmic microwave background that they think could be "bruises" from other universes bouncing off ours. They will be analyzing new data from the Planck satellite over the next few years to see if these patterns are real and if they are indicative of other universes. Also, a "dark flow" of galaxies in a particular direction has been discovered in an extremity of the visible portion of our universe that could be a gravitational pull from another universe. NASA is analyzing WMAP satellite data to further investigate this galaxy flow.

Cosmologists estimate there are about 500 billion galaxies in our universe. Our Milky Way galaxy is estimated to contain between 200 billion and 400 billion stars, of which our sun is just one. The Milky Way's neighboring Andromeda galaxy is estimated to contain over a trillion stars. Many stars have planets circling them and many planets have one or more moons. Our sun has eight planets circling it, so there could easily be billions of planets and moons just in our Milky Way galaxy with the possibility of life on many of them. By the end of 2011, NASA's planet-hunting Kepler satellite has identified 2,326 potential planets in its first sixteen months of operation. It has also confirmed the discovery of its first planet in a star's habitable zone—the just-right range of distance that could allow liquid water to exist. While the 2,326 potential planets are only candidates, it is expected that 80 to 90 percent of them will ultimately be confirmed as true planets. The region Kepler is investigating includes some 156,000 stars in what amounts to only one-four-hundredth of the sky in the Milky Way galaxy. The number of planet candidates is expected to grow substantially as we methodically search for them. The Kepler satellite is expected to examine these 156,000 stars between 2009 and 2013. By 2020 it is estimated that an additional 20,000 planets will have been found.

Statistically, it is probable that there are many Earth-like planets. Mathematically, based on 500 billion ($5 \times 10^{11}$) galaxies and conservatively assuming 100 billion stars per galaxy, we get $5 \times 10^{22}$ stars in the universe. Latest estimates made in 2010 by astrophysicists on the number of stars in our universe are much higher at 300 sextillion stars; that's $3 \times 10^{23}$ stars, of which our sun is just one. Based on the distribution of stars by mass in a galaxy, we can estimate that about 30% of the stars are solar-like. While it is difficult to estimate the percentage of solar-like stars that could have developed planetary systems, we do know it is greater than 0% and less than 100%. For purposes of this discussion, assume 10% of solar-like stars could have planetary systems. How many planets in these systems could be Earth-like in mass, in distance from their star, in atmosphere, etc? We don't know; however, from geological knowledge of the formation of our atmosphere, we do know that there is some probability—perhaps 1%. If we put all these conditions together we have, from these statistical considerations, $9 \times 10^{19}$ Earth-like planets in our universe. Even if you were to be far more conservative in estimating the number of Earth-like planets, the statistical likelihood is that there are many of them. Astronomer Carl Sagan suggested a number close to ten million just in the Milky Way galaxy. Based on Kepler satellite data in November 2011, two billion Earth-like planets are estimated just in our Milky Way galaxy. Scientists at NASA's Jet Propulsion Laboratory in Pasadena, California, focused on roughly Earth-size planets within habitable zones of their stars—that is, orbits where liquid water can exist on the surface of those worlds.

Seven factors that contribute to the probability that intelligent life exists in other worlds were suggested by Frank Drake, a professor of astronomy at the San Diego campus of the University of California. Combining all seven factors to estimate the number of technological alien societies that might exist provides the basis for a rough guess. Drake and other scientists have attempted to place upper and lower bounds on the probability of an alien society. Drake's lower bound for the Milky Way galaxy was in the order of 500 technological alien societies, and his upper bound was in the order of 150 million. The bottom line is that it is only a matter of time before we find an Earth-like planet in a habitable zone within our Milky Way galaxy. With this in mind, many cosmologists believe there is a good chance that past or present alien life of some form will be found in our solar system by the year 2025 and that a past or present technological alien society will be discovered within our galaxy by 2050.

**The M51 (NGC 5194), "Whirlpool" Spiral Galaxy**
Retrieved from:
http://hubblesite.org/gallery/album/pr2005012a/

Credit: NASA, ESA, S. Beckwith (STScl), and the Hubble Heritage Team (STScl/AURA).

**Centaurus A (NGC 5128), an Elliptical Galaxy**

Retrieved from:
http://hubblesite.org/gallery/album/pr2011018a/

Credit: NASA, ESA, and the Hubble Heritage (STScl/AURA)-ESA/Hubble Collaboration.

Space exploration has boosted knowledge of our universe many fold since the launch of the first man-made satellite. Far-reaching information gatherers, including the Hubble Space Telescope and various radio and infrared telescopes, have enabled us to see almost to the extremities of our visible universe 13.7 billion light years away. You can view many more amazing photos like Centaurus-A and M51 on the Internet taken by the Hubble Space Telescope at http://hubblesite.org/gallery/album.

Outside of our solar system, it is difficult to impossible to see planets. Instead they are identified by the effect they have on the respective star they orbit. Our solar system resides in the pin-wheel shaped Milky Way galaxy about 30,000 light years distance from the galaxy core. The Milky Way galaxy has six spiral arms: Norma, Scutum-Crux, Sagittarius, Orion, Perseus, and Cygnus. Our solar system is on the inner rim of Orion one-half to two-thirds of the way from the center of the galaxy. The Orion Arm is not a major spiral arm but only an enhancement of stars and gas between the Sagittarius and Perseus arms. It should be emphasized that there are almost as many stars between the spiral arms as in the spiral arms. The reason why the arms of spiral galaxies are so prominent is that the brightest stars are found in the spiral arms. Spiral arms are the major regions of star formation in spiral galaxies, and this is where most of the major nebulae are found. The Milky Way galaxy itself is roughly 80,000 light years in diameter and 16,000 light years thick at its core, and it is about 3,000 light years thick in the spiral arm where our solar system resides.

**Milky Way, a Spiral Galaxy**

Retrieved from:
http://www.atlasoftheuniverse.com/milkyway.html

The night sky is a myriad of stars to human eyes. Powerful telescopes show us the remote planets and galaxies we cannot see with our eyes. Many objects are too cool to give off visible light, which represents only a tiny sliver of the electromagnetic spectrum. These objects, however, emit energy in an invisible form of longer wavelengths known as infrared radiation. Incredibly hot objects, like massive exploding stars called supernovas, give off much of their energy in shorter wavelengths in the form of gamma rays and X-rays not visible to our eyes.

Earth gets hit by a massive dose of gamma radiation about once every 100 million years. Such blasts contribute to the depletion of the Earth's ozone layer. Disruption of the ozone layer lets ultraviolet light filter down to the surface of the Earth, where it can change organisms by mutating their genes. Destruction of the ozone layer can have many effects on life on our planet. Gamma radiation blasts on the world's plants and animals can wreak havoc on Earth's food webs. Such blasts most likely led to some of the Earth's past extinction events.

Light travels at 186,282 miles per second; therefore, if you multiply 186,282 miles per second by the number of seconds in a year (31,536,000), and then multiply that by 13.73 billion years, you will get the approximate distance in miles in any direction that can be viewed via various methods ($8.06 \times 10^{22}$ miles). The portion of our universe within the time horizon that can be viewed is mind-boggling, and that is just a fraction of the total. It is important to understand that the further out we look, the further back in time we see. Because of this, astronomers are able to piece together an outline of our universe's history stretching backward from the present by observing the nature of objects at ever greater distances from the Earth. We can see stars coming into existence and others reaching the end of their existence; however, by the time we see them, because of their great distance, millions and perhaps billions of years may have passed since the actual events took place. Creation and destruction are ongoing evolutionary processes within our universe. In talking about creation and destruction of stars, one must remember Einstein's equation $e = mc^2$. Energy (e) and mass (m) are related to each other by the speed of light (c) squared. When stars cease to exist their energy/mass are conserved within our universe and lead to the formation of new stars.

While our universe has evolved over time, so too has the understanding of our universe. At one time Earth was considered to be the center of the universe. It was thought that all that was visible in the sky rotated around Earth. From careful observations of the night sky, the Greeks envisioned a spherical Earth at the center of our universe, surrounded by concentric spheres on which planets were fixed, with the outermost sphere containing stars and beyond that the "external fire." In the third century BC, Aristarchus of Samos proposed a sun-centered universe. In the second century BC, Ptolemy proposed an Earth-centered universe with the sun and the planets revolving around Earth. This view remained unchanged until the sixteenth century, in part because it became interwoven with Christian theology.

New views emerged through the work of people such as Copernicus, Kepler, Galileo, and Newton. In the early sixteenth century, Copernicus, a Polish astronomer, advanced the theory that Earth and other planets revolved around the sun. Copernicus was a devout Catholic and his theory was in conflict with the teachings of the Catholic Church. He withheld his theory for many years for fear of objections from the Pope. Kepler, a German astronomer and mathematician in the beginning of the seventeenth century, carried Copernicus' theory further, stating elliptical orbits of planets around the sun.

It was not until Galileo Galilei turned his newly made telescope to the stars in the fall of 1609 that he saw the Milky Way as a "congeries of innumerable stars." Later he saw the pock-marked surface of the moon "full of cavities and prominences." Then he observed that Jupiter had "four moons" and that Venus had "moonlike phases." He later saw imperfections in the sun. Galileo proved that Earth was not the center of the universe, as had been believed since the third century BC, but instead that the sun was the center of our solar system (which since the third century BC had been equated to be the universe).

After 1610, when he began publicly supporting the heliocentric (sun-centered) view, Galileo met with bitter opposition from some philosophers and clerics, and two of the latter eventually denounced him to the Roman Inquisition (a system of tribunals developed by the Pope early in 1615). Although he was cleared of any offence at that time, in February 1616 the Catholic Church nevertheless condemned heliocentrism as "false and contrary to Scripture," and Galileo was warned to abandon his support for it, which he promised to do. When he later defended his views in his most famous work, *Dialogue Concerning the Two Chief World Systems*, published in 1632, he was tried by the Inquisition, found "vehemently suspect of heresy," forced to recant, and spent the rest of his life under house arrest.

Isaac Newton, an English mathematician and scientist who invented differential calculus, formulated the theory of universal gravitation presented in his *Principia Mathematica* in 1687. Newton postulated the laws of motion. He described how gravity affected the planets using mathematics. He stated how planets fall toward the sun and yet maintain their distance due to their orbital speed.

Throughout the seventeenth and early eighteenth centuries, astronomers used telescopes to steadily improve maps and tables depicting the positions and motions of stars and planets. To penetrate deeper into the heavens, they built telescopes with bigger lenses for more light gathering and longer focal lengths for greater magnification. In 1864, William Huggins attached a prism to his telescope such that it broke the light received into a rainbow spectrum and thus was able to reveal the physical state and chemical composition of an object emitting its own light. Incredibly, one could determine what stars were made of by analyzing the rainbow spectrum of their starlight.

Albert Einstein provided the next big leap in understanding our universe. In 1905 he published his *Special Theory of Relativity*, positing that space and time are not separate continuums but instead are one space-time continuum, and in 1915 he published his *General Theory of Relativity*, showing that an energy density warps the space-time continuum. Einstein taught us that space and time can be combined into space-time, which has the ability to evolve and grow. Indeed, what we think of as gravity is just a manifestation of the curvature of space-time. To find things in the universe, including dark matter and dark energy, all we have to do is to map out this curvature. The expansion of the universe is governed by its spatial curvature and energy density, both of which have specific ways of changing as the universe grows.

Dark matter is thought to make up much of the universe, but scientists have little idea what it is. They can only infer the existence of dark matter by measuring its gravitational tug on the normal matter that they can see. The idea of dark matter was first proposed in the 1930s, after the velocities of galaxies and stars suggested the universe contained much more mass than what could be seen. Dark matter would not reflect light, so it couldn't be observed directly by telescopes. One way to detect dark matter is to use light as a probe of the gravitational field. Passing through curved space-time, the path of a light ray is deflected due to gravitational lensing. This lensing demonstrates the existence of gravitational fields where there is essentially no ordinary matter. These features are related to each other by Einstein's general theory of relativity, which can be used to model the past and possible future of the universe.

In 2003, NASA's Wilkinson Microwave Anisotropy Probe (WMAP) satellite took detailed pictures of the cosmic microwave background proving there was a "hot" Big Bang. From these images it was determined that our universe is $13.73 \pm 0.12$ billion years old (within 1 percent error). The WMAP satellite also confirmed that our universe is inflating. Thus, today we have what we call the Inflationary Hot Big Bang Theory.

While our universe is expanding at an increasing rate, our understanding of the universe is also expanding at an increasing rate. This can be seen from a "Timeline of Cosmological Theories and Discoveries" included at the end of this chapter. With the advent of the computer followed by our ventures into space and the hundreds of man-made satellites gathering information, we have learned more about our universe in the last century than in all previous years since the beginning of mankind.

On April 24, 1990, the space shuttle *Discovery* carried the Hubble Space Telescope into space and, on April 27, 1990, released it into orbit. The Hubble has profoundly transformed our understanding of our universe. It has provided us with dazzling images of our universe and has shown new and unexpected aspects of our universe. The Hubble Space Telescope is perhaps the most productive scientific instrument ever created by humans. The images and data gleaned from Hubble observations have provided clues to some of the most fundamental questions in science. It has captured star births and deaths, galactic collisions, and the accelerating expansion of our universe. It added to the evidence for black holes at the center of galaxies in the 1990s by measuring how quickly the innermost parts of galaxies rotate—up to 1.1 million miles per hour in big galaxies. These speeds pointed to galaxy cores containing up to a billion times the mass of our sun. The discovery that super-massive black holes are at the core of galaxies is one of the Hubble's greatest achievements. In 2002 it was determined by scientists at the Keck observatory that near the Milky Way's black hole a star's top speed was about 20 million miles per hour.

In 2018, barring unforeseen problems (including funding), the James Webb Space Telescope will be launched. It will be a large, infrared-optimized space telescope. Webb will find the first galaxies that formed in the early universe, connecting the Big Bang to our own Milky Way galaxy. It will peer through dusty clouds to see stars forming planetary systems, connecting the Milky Way to our own solar system. Webb's instruments will be designed to work primarily in the infrared range of the electromagnetic spectrum, with some capability in the visible range. It will be stationed more than a million miles away from Earth. The primary mirror is 6.5 meters in diameter and so will offer a much bigger light-collecting area than the Hubble's 2.4-meter mirror. The Hubble has led to some of the shining achievements of our civilization. The Webb will build on these achievements and greatly expand our ability to understand our universe. It will provide more detailed information on how the universe works at the farthest reaches of space.

The Hubble telescope was designed to view the near ultraviolet, visible, and near infrared, which is only a small part of the overall electromagnetic spectrum. The Compton observatory was launched in 1991 to observe gamma rays, while Chandra was launched in 1999 to study the X-ray spectrum, and Spitzer was launched in 2003 to study the infrared spectrum. Compton fell to

Earth in 2000 and was replaced by Fermi in 2008. Much has been learned about our universe by looking at different ranges of the electromagnetic spectrum. In recent years extraordinary space missions have found water on Mars, magnetic storms on Mercury, and volcanoes on the moons of Saturn. A "Timeline of Artificial Satellites and Space Probes," from Wikipedia, is included at the end of this chapter.

Discoveries in astronomy and physics have shown beyond a reasonable doubt that our universe did, in fact, have a beginning. Prior to that moment our universe did not exist; during and after that moment our universe did exist. The Inflationary Hot Big Bang Theory pretty much explains what happened during and after that moment. According to the theory, our universe sprang into existence from a "singularity" around 13.73 billion years ago. Singularities defy our current understanding of physics. They exist at the core of black holes. Black holes are areas of intense gravitational pressure. The pressure is thought to be so intense that finite matter is actually squished into an infinite density (a concept which boggles the mind). These zones of infinite density are called "singularities." Our universe is thought to have begun as an infinitesimally small, infinitely hot, infinitely dense singularity. Where did it come from? We don't know. Why did it appear? We don't know. We do know, however, that at the center of most galaxies and perhaps all galaxies is a massive black hole and at the core of a black hole is a singularity.

After its initial appearance, our universe expanded and cooled, going from very, very small and very, very hot to the size and temperature of our current universe. It continues to expand and cool to this day and we are inside of it: incredible creatures living on a unique planet, circling a beautiful star clustered together with several hundred billion other stars in a galaxy soaring through an expanding universe along with billions of other galaxies, all of which began as an infinitesimal singularity which appeared out of nowhere for reasons unknown. This is the Inflationary Hot Big Bang Theory.

There are many misconceptions surrounding the Big Bang Theory. For example, we tend to imagine a giant explosion. Astrophysicists, however, say that there was no explosion; there was (and continues to be) a rapid expansion. Rather than imagining a balloon popping and releasing its contents, imagine a balloon expanding: an infinitesimally small balloon expanding to the size of our current universe. Another misconception is that we tend to imagine a singularity as a little fireball appearing somewhere in space. Some experts believe space didn't exist prior to the Inflationary Hot Big Bang. On the other hand, many believe that the cosmos is infinite in time and space and that our universe is expanding into that space.

Some cosmologists believe that because singularities are at the core of black holes and since our universe emerged from a singularity, it is likely that other universes have emerged from similar singularities such that our cosmos consists of many universes. Our particular universe contains many galaxies with massive black holes as their cores. Maybe other such universes exist, and perhaps new universes have been born from those black holes such that there are universes within universes. Maybe our universe will someday become the parent of future universes.

Our universe perhaps is one of many in the cosmos with energy from other universes pulling on our universe causing our universe to expand. This is an alternative to the usual theory that our universe is accelerating because of the dark energy within it. Could it be that our universe is within another universe and its gravitational pull on our universe is what we are calling dark energy? Possibly someday cosmologists and astrophysicists will be able to prove or disprove this idea. At this time, however, we cannot detect anything further out than 13.7 billion light years distant, so we cannot directly detect other universes.

Back in the late 1960s and early 1970s, when men first walked upon the moon, three British astrophysicists, Steven Hawking, George Ellis, and Roger Penrose, turned their attention to the Theory of Relativity and its implications regarding our notions of time. In 1968 and 1970, they published papers in which they extended Einstein's Theory of General Relativity to include measurements of time and space. According to their calculations, time and space, with respect to our universe, had a finite beginning that corresponds to the origin of our universe's matter and energy. A conclusion was that the singularity didn't appear in space; rather, space began inside of the singularity. Prior to the singularity, our universe did not exist—not its space, time, matter, or energy. So where and in what did the singularity appear if not in space? Cosmologists don't know. They don't know where it came from, why it's here, or even where it is. All they really know is that we are inside of it and at one time it didn't exist and neither did we.

While the space of our universe did begin inside of a singularity, some believe the singularity formed within the space of a black hole in an existing cosmos infinite in time and space. Hopefully this idea will be proven true or false at some point in the near future. Perhaps it was a quantum fluctuation in an existing cosmos that triggered the Inflationary Hot Big Bang. If one such quantum fluctuation lasted sufficiently long and achieved the right conditions, it could have subsequently undergone inflation, with our universe becoming what it is today. If that fluctuation grew according to Inflation Theory and that growth conserves energy, it still has essentially zero energy. No new energy would be created at all. So, effectively, we have a universe from nothing. And yes, the total energy of our universe appears to be zero or extremely close to it. Matter, antimatter, and photons together appear to have an equal amount of energy but opposite in sign to the gravitational energy associated with them.

What are the major evidences which support the Big Bang Theory? First of all, we are now certain our universe had a beginning. Secondly, galaxies are moving away from us at speeds proportional to their distance. This is called Hubble's Law, named after Edwin Hubble (1889-1953), who discovered this phenomenon in 1929. This observation supports the expansion of the universe and suggests the universe was once compacted. Thirdly, if the universe was initially very, very hot, as the Big Bang suggests, we should be able to find some remnant of this heat. In 1965, radio astronomers Arno Penzias and Robert Wilson discovered a 2.725 degree Kelvin (-454.765 degree Fahrenheit, -270.425 degree Celsius) Cosmic Microwave Background (CMB) radiation that pervades the observable universe. This is the remnant for which scientists were looking. Penzias and Wilson shared in the 1978 Nobel Prize for physics for their discovery.

They were working for Bell Labs, researching microwave radiation in our universe. What they found was that, while there were interesting microwave emissions from the plane of our galaxy, there was this low-temperature noise everywhere that they simply couldn't get rid of. They were puzzled by it, but cosmologists knew exactly what it was. It was the CMB remnant heat from the Big Bang that had been predicted by George Gamow and his students in the 1940s.

**The 50-foot Holmdel horn antenna at Bell labs in Holmdel, New Jersey, USA, with which Arno Penzias and Robert Wilson discovered cosmic microwave background radiation in 1964.** *(Photo Credit: Bell Labs)*

Retrieved from:
http://nps.gov/history/history/online_books/butowsky5/images/astro4k.jpg

The CMB is a view of the universe 400,000 years after the Big Bang. Prior to this time the young universe consisted of just protons, electrons, neutrons, and photons in the form of a hot foggy ionized gas. We know from the CMB that the ionized gas was 75% hydrogen and 25% helium. Expansion cooled the universe, and after 400,000 years the temperature dropped below 3,000 degrees Kelvin, at which point conditions were calm enough for electrons to be caught and held by protons whereby atoms formed and the fog cleared. The abundance of the "light elements," hydrogen and helium, found in the observable universe, support the Big Bang model of origins. The helium abundance tells us the temperature of our universe was about 100 million degrees Kelvin at about three minutes into its existence.

The physics of what occurs in a black hole is not completely understood, but scientists are working on it using such tools as the Large Hadron Collider at CERN, the giant laboratory just outside of Geneva on the border of Switzerland and France. The Large Hadron Collider can recreate the conditions of the Big Bang at 1/100 of a picosecond, when the temperature was 100 million billion degrees Kelvin.

The Large Hadron Collider is the world's largest and highest-energy particle accelerator. It was built at a cost of $10 billion and resides in a 17-mile-round ring of tunnels at a depth ranging from 160 feet to 574 feet beneath the French-Swiss border. The machine can accelerate protons up to 99.999999% of the speed of light through two channels running in opposite directions whereby the protons are collided head-on. Billions of bits of data can be sent out every second for analysis of the collisions. The collider was built to address questions such as: what was the new-born universe made of; what causes things to have mass; why is most of the mass hidden; can we provide a unified theory for the four forces of nature; where did all the antimatter go when the universe came into existence; and is our universe a mere sliver of all that there is. The four known fundamental forces of nature are electromagnetism, strong interaction, weak interaction (also known as strong and weak nuclear forces), and gravitation.

At the end of the 1960s, a theory was proposed that unified the weak nuclear force with electromagnetism. Experiments in the 1970s and 1980s confirmed the electroweak theory. In 1979, Steven Weinberg, Sheldon Glashow, and Abdus Salam received the Nobel Prize in physics for unifying the weak nuclear interaction with electromagnetism. Hopefully, the Large Hadron Collider can help us answer many questions as it comes very close to recreating the Big Bang on an extremely small scale. While astronomers and cosmologists are looking outward, physicists are looking inward into atomic particles to better understand our universe and its origin. The Large Hadron Collider should help us better understand black holes and our universe's evolution.

One of the most interesting theories in particle physics of the last 25 years has been the suggestion of a particle called the Higgs boson—a hypothetical massive elementary particle predicted to exist by the Standard Model of particle physics. Postulated as a means of resolving inconsistencies in the Standard Model, it is predicted to have a mass about 125 times the mass of a proton, and it would fill in the last missing piece of a puzzle involving the solution of one of the great outstanding problems in physics of the twentieth century: the origin of all mass. Experiments attempting to find the Higgs particle using the Large Hadron Collider have been somewhat successful. As of December 2011, scientists have found evidence that could be indicative of the Higgs boson, but more data is needed before they can declare a true discovery. They anticipate they will know by the end of 2012. If the Higgs boson is confirmed, that could totally change the way we see the universe. In the far future, we might even find a way to take advantage of the Higgs field, just as earlier physicists took advantage of the electromagnetic field, radioactivity, and quantum effects.

The Standard Model of particle physics provides a description of microscopic matter and their fundamental interactions. All matter is comprised of quarks and leptons. Three quarks bind to form the proton and neutron. The neutrons and protons stick together to form nuclei—the tiny, heavy central "hearts" of atoms. Leptons appear in nature in two types: electrically charged and neutral. Neutral leptons are called neutrinos and hardly interact with matter at all. There are three known charged leptons, the lightest of which is the electron. Electrons, which are negatively charged, are attracted to nuclei, which are positively charged, to form atoms. A good pictorial representation of an atom is a cloud of electrons swarming around a tiny nucleus, much the way bees might swarm around a queen who has left her hive. Since atoms make up everything in the world, quarks and leptons are the fundamental building blocks of nature.

As we come closer to developing an ultimate theory of the universe, how will this impact religion? As science explains more and more, there is less and less need for religious explanations. Originally, in the history of human beings, everything was mysterious. Fire, rain, birth, death—all seemed to require the action of some kind of divine being. As time has passed, we have explained more and more in a purely naturalistic way. Astronomers are now designing new observatories to probe the acceleration of our universe and other cosmic phenomena. Physicists are also looking forward to new experiments that will dramatically improve our understanding of particles and forces and how ordinary matter fits in with dark matter and dark energy. Understanding the universe in a naturalistic way doesn't contradict religion, but it does take away one of the original motivations for religion. If scientists put together something like a final theory in which the four forces of nature and atomic particles are explained, and that theory also sheds light on the origin of the Big Bang and gives a consistent picture of cosmology, there will be a little less for religion to explain. Most religions have stopped trying to explain nature religiously and have left that to science.

Aristotle told us Earth consisted of five elements: earth, air, fire, water, and ether. Modern cosmology recognizes five cosmic elements: atomic matter, dark matter, photons, neutrinos, and dark energy. Atomic matter only amounts to 4.6% of what the universe is made of; dark matter accounts for 23.3%; photons account for 0.005% (light is made of photons); neutrinos account for 0.0034%; and, dark energy accounts for 72.1%. The atomic matter that makes up the planets, stars, solar systems, galaxies, and even us only accounts for 4.6% of what the universe is made of. Dark matter and dark energy make up 95.4% of the universe. Atomic matter includes every kind of particle ever directly observed; dark matter consists of massive particles known only because of their gravitational effects; and dark energy is a smoothly distributed component whose density does not change as the universe expands. While we don't know much yet about dark matter and dark energy, a best guess is that dark matter is a kind of subatomic particle made in the Big Bang. We know that dark matter exists from its gravitational effects.

Armed with the core principles of particle physics, we know enough about the early universe to predict how many of each type of particle should be left over from the Big Bang. These "relic abundances" are crucial to understanding the origin of dark matter and light elements. Dark energy was discovered in 1998. Its nature is still unknown, but a best guess is that it is a residual energy associated with space itself, and for this reason it is some-times referred to as a vacuum energy. Dark energy might be the result of a non-perfect cancellation of quantum fluctuations—virtual particles created out of nothing as a consequence of quantum physics (specifically the Heisenberg Uncertainty Principle). Virtual particles spontaneously form out of nothing, existing for a short time and then annihilating each other.

The existence of dark energy is revealed by its gravitational effect. It is what makes the universe's expansion speed up. Einstein's famous equation, $e = mc^2$ (where e is energy, m is mass, and c is the speed of light), reminds us that the five cosmic elements (atomic matter, dark matter, photons, neutrinos, and dark energy) are just different versions of a single entity: energy. When we consider the constituents in the form of energy and add gravitational energy (a negative energy) to the list and consider the sum of their energy, we discover that the entire universe sums up to essentially zero energy—it sums to nothing. What this tells us is that perhaps the universe could have originated from nothing. Likely from some yet to be understood condition at the core of a black hole, our universe emerged—perhaps triggered by a quantum fluctuation.

At 380,000 years of age, atoms of hydrogen and helium began to form from the ionized gas making up our universe. Slight variations in density throughout the universe led to the formation of stars. The denser areas had more mass, which pro-vided for greater gravitational attraction, thus causing an accretion process (the growth by gravitationally attracting more matter) to occur, forming the first stars. The first stars consisted of pure hydrogen and helium. They became very massive and very hot and powerful, perhaps a million times brighter than our sun. Deep in the heart of these massive stars the conditions were such that thermonuclear fusion eventually took place, building heavier nuclei from lighter ones. As stars age, heavier nuclei come to the surface where the nuclei gain their electrons to become full atoms. Depending on how a star dies, these atoms are ejected calmly or explosively into space, where they may drift for several billion years before forming a denser gas cloud by amassing with other atoms and forming into new stars and planets.

As the mass of a star increases, its core becomes hotter and heavier elements can be formed. Even with some heavier elements, stars are still mostly made up of hydrogen and helium. Almost all heavenly bodies contain three-fourths hydrogen, one-fourth helium, and 0 – 4% heavier elements. Earth is an exception as its relatively weak gravity does not retain hydrogen and helium very well. We know from the heavier elements of the sun (via spectrometry) that it is a third-generation star. First generation stars consist of lighter elements such as helium. As stars become supernovas and explode, heavier elements are formed. New stars are formed from the remnants of past stars. The more generations of stars that pass, the greater amount of heavier elements come into existence replacing lighter elements—an evolutionary process.

The sun is at the center of our solar system. About three-quarters of the sun's mass consists of hydrogen, while the rest is mostly helium. Less than 2% consists of heavier elements, including oxygen, carbon, neon, iron, and others. The sun formed about 4.6 billion years ago and the eight planets in our solar system followed shortly thereafter. The sun and its eight orbiting planets all formed over a period of about 50 million years.

Earth is the third planet from our sun in the Milky Way galaxy. It is the densest and fifth largest of the eight planets in our solar system. It is also the largest of our solar system's four terrestrial planets (the remaining four are gaseous). About 70.8% of Earth's surface is covered by water. Earth formed by accretion from the solar nebula. A nebula is an interstellar cloud of dust, hydrogen gas, helium gas, and other ionized gases. Earth is a very special place as it lies in a star-centered orbit at a distance from the sun, where it can maintain liquid water on its surface. This area is called the habitable zone, an area where life forms can exist.

Most of the water on Earth came from constant bombardment by comets. Around 4.1 billion years ago began a period of heavy bombardment when Earth was pummeled by comets and cold meteorites—both of which carry water. This heavy bombardment ended about 3.8 billion years ago, and at that point much of the Earth's water was in place, setting the stage for the earliest forms of microbial life about 3.6 billion years ago. Comets consist of ice and cosmic dust, and they melt as they pass into Earth's upper atmosphere, producing a continual rain of water to our planet's surface. Comets several kilometers wide are readily seen in the sky. As many as 15 million smaller ones, less than twelve meters in diameter, pelt Earth's atmosphere every year.

Several steps led to the formation of the planets from a rotating cosmic dust cloud. When the dust cloud reached a certain density and rate of rotation, it flattened into a disk, and the material of the disk then segregated into rings and then later condensed into gaseous and solid clumps. Many of these clumps subsequently coalesced to form the eight planets of our solar system while others remain as asteroids. This aggregation process still continues today. Earth currently receives an estimated 100,000 tons of meteorites and particles annually. Earth formed 4.5672 billion years ago.

Our moon was formed shortly after Earth's initial accretion from a glancing blow by a now non-existent planet posthumously named Theia, a body probably about the size of Mars (one-tenth of Earth's mass). The collision occurred about 4.533 billion years ago when the planet hit the Earth at an oblique angle and was destroyed in the process. The collision also caused the Earth to tilt on its axis by 15°, causing our seasons. The throttling was so severe scientists believe Earth melted. The mantle of Theia and a significant portion of the Earth's silicate mantle were thrust into space, resulting in rings around the young Earth which lasted for millions of years until they coalesced to form the moon. It is the gravitational pull of the moon which stabilized the Earth's fluctuating axis of rotation, leading to a relatively stable climate. This was important for setting up the conditions for the formation of life on Earth. If Earth had no moon or a much smaller moon, our climate would be much less stable. Some stabilization would be provided by the gravitational pull of Jupiter, albeit much less effect than what our moon provides, and therefore our climate would reach further extremes.

Our Earth is a very special place. In just the past 750 million years it has gone through remarkable changes. Continents have shifted, ice ages have come and gone, sea levels have risen and fallen, and one-time deserts have turned green, allowing creatures to crawl out of the oceans and live on the land. While the distribution of land mass among the continents has changed dramatically, the total land area has stayed relatively constant.

The next twenty years in cosmology promise to be no less interesting than the last. New experiments are in the works to deepen our understanding in six areas: dark matter, dark energy, the universe's first billion years, galaxy evolution, inflation, and the early universe.

So what will be the fate of our universe? We know we live in a universe that is accelerating in its expansion. Assuming it will expand forever, stars will burn out, leaving behind white dwarfs, brown dwarfs, neutron stars, and other degenerate objects. After a very long time, the material in these objects will disintegrate as all the protons decay into other particles leaving black holes. These, too, will evaporate eventually, leaving a cold, vast, nearly empty space consisting of only electrons, positrons, neutrinos, and extremely low-energy photons.

# Timeline for our Universe

| | |
|---|---|
| $10^{-43}$ seconds | Temperature was about $10^{32}$ ° K. |
| $10^{-35}$ seconds | Temperature was about $10^{28}$ ° K. Universe was inflating exponentially fast, stretching space to make it flat and giving it the same properties everywhere. (Saying that space is flat means that it is not curved in any direction. As such, if you were to pick any three points in space and connect them to form a triangle, the three angles will always add up to 180 degrees.) |
| $10^{-30}$ seconds | All the energy that was stored in space causing the exponential expansion became an incredibly dense bath of hot particles of matter, anti-matter, and radiation. |
| $10^{-30}$ - $10^{-10}$ secs. | Natural processes created slightly more matter than anti-matter in our universe. Even though there is only about one extra matter particle for every one billion pairs of matter-antimatter particles, that's enough to explain all the matter in our universe. Most of the matter combined with antimatter, leaving only a slight excess of matter. This process is called baryogenesis. |
| $10^{-12}$ seconds | Gas temperatures were about $10^{16}$ ° K. We can reproduce the behavior of matter at this temperature with particle accelerators. |
| $10^{-6}$ seconds | Temperature was about $10^{13}$ ° K. |
| 1 second | Temperature was about 10 billion ($10^{10}$) ° K. Conditions in the universe were similar to that of the cores of stars for which we know the abundance of their various elements. A sea of photons formed that eventually became the Cosmic Microwave Background. |

| | |
|---|---|
| 3 minutes | After all the antimatter annihilated away with the matter, there was a little bit of matter left over in a sea of radiation, and then our universe cooled enough so that protons and neutrons could fuse together to form heavier nuclei without being blasted apart. This is when nearly all the hydrogen, deuterium, helium, and lithium in our universe were created (about 75% hydrogen, about 25% helium, and the rest less than 0.01%). This process is called nucleosynthesis. The helium abundance tells us it was about 100 million ° K at 3 minutes. |
| 380,000 years | The first neutral atoms formed. Up until this point, all of the radiation energy in the universe was too cold to blast the nuclei of atoms apart, but that energy was also too hot to allow neutral atoms to form. It took almost 400,000 years for the universe to expand and cool enough for the leftover radiation from the Big Bang to cool down. Finally, at this point, electrons and nuclei formed into neutral atoms. When this happened, the leftover radiation flew off in all directions, which we can detect today as the Cosmic Microwave Background. The Cosmic Microwave Background tells us that everywhere in the universe was about 3000° K at 400,000 years. |
| 50 million years | The first stars in the universe began to form. These first stars were huge, hundreds or even thousands of times as massive as our sun, and consisted of hydrogen and helium. It took about 50 million years for gravity to collapse matter into volumes dense enough and massive enough to ignite nuclear fusion. The intense heat from the nuclear fusion caused the hydrogen and helium atoms to |

fuse into successively heavier elements, including carbon, with the heaviest being iron. (Iron is the last nuclear fusion reaction that is exothermic, becoming the last element to be produced before collapse of a supernova.) These stars all ended as supernovae or even hyper novae, with the intense heat of these exploding stars causing further fusion of atoms creating even heavier elements than iron, and their remnants were spread all over the universe.

1 - 2 billion years — Star groups merged to form infant elliptical galaxies. There were frequent galaxy collisions, high star birth rates, and high supernova rates.

8 billion years — Spiral-like galaxies began to form.

9.1 billion years — Our Sun and solar system formed in the disk of the Milky Way galaxy. Earth and the other planets in our solar system formed at almost the same time. Earth is 4.5672 billion years old $\pm$ 0.0006 billion years.

13.73 billion years — Today.

# Timeline of Cosmological Theories and Discoveries

(From Wikipedia—the on-line dictionary)

| Years | Theory/Discovery |
|---|---|
| 3rd century BC | Aristarchus of Samos proposes a sun-centered universe. |
| 2nd century AD | Ptolemy proposes an Earth-centered Universe, with the sun and planets revolving around Earth. |
| 5th century on | Several astronomers (including Aryabhata, Bhaskara I, Ibn al-Shatir, and Copernicus) propose a sun-centered universe. |
| 1576 | Thomas Digges modifies the Copernican system by removing the outer edge and replacing it with a star-filled unbounded space. |
| 1584 | Giordano Bruno proposes a non-hierarchical cosmology, wherein the Copernican solar system is not the center of the universe, but rather, a relatively insignificant star system, amongst an infinite multitude of others. |
| 1610 | Johannes Kepler uses the dark night sky to argue for a finite universe. |
| 1687 | Isaac Newton's laws describe large-scale motion throughout the universe. |
| 1720 | Edmund Halley puts forth an early form of Olbers' paradox (the argument that the darkness of the night sky conflicts with the supposition of an infinite and eternal static universe). The paradox is one of the pieces of evidence for a non-static universe, such as the current Big-Bang model. |
| 1744 | Jean-Philippe de Cheseaux puts forth an early form of Olbers' paradox. |
| 1791 | Erasmus Darwin pens the first description of a cyclical expanding and contracting universe. |

| | |
|---|---|
| 1826 | Heinrich Wilhelm Olbers puts forth Olbers' paradox. |
| 1848 | Edgar Allan Poe offers first correct solution to Olbers' paradox in an essay that also suggests the expansion and collapse of the universe. |
| 1905 | Albert Einstein publishes the Special Theory of Relativity, positing that space and time are not separate continuums. |
| 1915 | Albert Einstein publishes the General Theory of Relativity, showing that an energy density warps space-time. |
| 1917 | Willem de Sitter derives an isotropic static cosmology with a cosmological constant as well as an empty expanding cosmology with a cosmological constant, termed a de Sitter universe. |
| 1922 | Vesto Slipher summarizes his findings on the spiral nebulae's systematic redshifts. |
| 1922 | Alexander Friedmann finds a solution to the Einstein field equations which suggests a general expansion of space. |
| 1927 | Georges Lemaitre discusses the creation event of an expanding universe governed by the Einstein field equations. |
| 1928 | Howard Percy Robertson briefly mentions that Vesto Slipher's redshift measurements combined with brightness measurements of the same galaxies indicate a redshift-distance relation. |
| 1929 | Edwin Hubble demonstrates the linear redshift-distance relation and thus shows the expansion of the universe. |
| 1933 | Edward Milne names and formalizes the cosmological principle. |
| 1934 | Georges Lemaitre interprets the cosmological constant as due to a vacuum energy with an unusual perfect fluid equation of state. |

| | |
|---|---|
| 1938 | Paul Dirac suggests the Large Numbers Hypothesis, that the gravitational constant may be small because it is decreasing slowly with time. |
| 1948 | Ralph Alpher, Hans Bethe (in absentia), and George Gamow examine element synthesis in a rapidly expanding and cooling universe and suggest that the elements were produced by rapid neutron capture. |
| 1948 | Hermann Bondi, Thomas Gold, and Fred Hoyle propose steady state cosmologies based on the perfect cosmological principal. |
| 1948 | George Gamow predicts the existence of the cosmic microwave background radiation by considering the behavior of primordial radiation in an expanding universe. |
| 1950 | Fred Hoyle derisively coins the term "Big Bang." |
| 1961 | Robert Dicke argues that carbon-based life can only arise when the gravitational force is small, because this is when burning stars exist; this is the first use of the weak anthropic principle. |
| 1965 | Hannes Alfven proposes the now-discounted concept of ambiplasma to explain baryon asymmetry. |
| 1965 | Martin Rees and Dennis Sciama analyze quasar source count data and discover that the quasar density increases with redshift. |
| 1965 | Arno Penzias and Robert Wilson, astronomers at Bell Labs, discover the $2.7°K$ microwave background radiation, which earns them the 1978 Nobel Prize in physics. Robert Dicke, James Peebles, Peter Roll, and David Todd Wilkinson interpret it as a relic from the Big Bang. |
| 1966 | Stephen Hawking and George Ellis show that any plausible general relativistic cosmology is singular. |

| 1966 | James Peebles shows that the Hot Big Bang predicts the correct helium abundance. |
| 1967 | Andrei Sakharov presents the requirements for baryogenesis, a baryon-antibaryon asymmetry in the universe. |
| 1967 | John Bahcall/ Wal Sargent, and Maarten Schmidt measure the fine-structure splitting of spectral lines in the quasar 3C191 and thereby show that the fine-structure constant does not vary significantly with time. |
| 1968 | Brandon Carter speculates that perhaps the fundamental constants of nature must lie within a restricted range to allow the emergence of life; this is the first use of the strong anthropic principle. |
| 1969 | Charles Misner formally presents the Big Bang horizon problem. |
| 1969 | Robert Dicke formally presents the Big Bang flatness problem. |
| 1969 | Humans walk on the moon. |
| 1973 | Edward Tryon proposes that the universe may be a large-scale quantum mechanical vacuum fluctuation where positive mass-energy is balanced by negative gravitational potential energy. |
| 1974 | Robert Wagoner, William Fowler, and Fred Hoyle show that the Hot Big Bang predicts the correct deuterium and lithium abundances. |
| 1976 | Alex Shlyakhter uses samarium ratios from the Oklo prehistoric natural nuclear fission reactor in Gabon, Africa to show that some laws of physics have remained unchanged for over two billion years. |
| 1977 | Gary Steigman, David Schramm, and James Gunn examine the relation between the primordial helium abundance and number of |

|       |                                                                                 |
|-------|---------------------------------------------------------------------------------|
|       | neutrinos and claim that at most five lepton families can exist.                |
| 1981  | Viacheslav Mukhanov and G. Chibisov propose that quantum fluctuations could lead to large scale structure in an inflationary universe. |
| 1990  | Preliminary results from NASA's COBE (**CO**smic **B**ackground Explorer) mission confirm the cosmic microwave background radiation is an isotropic blackbody to an astonishing one part in $10^5$ precision, thus eliminating the possibility of an integrated starlight model proposed for the background by steady state enthusiasts. |
| 1990s | Ground based cosmic microwave background experiments determine that the universe is geometrically flat. |
| 1998  | Controversial evidence for the fine structure constant varying over the lifetime of the universe is first published. |
| 1998  | Adam Riess, Saul Perlmutter and others discover the cosmic acceleration in observations of Type Ia supernovae, providing the first evidence for a non-zero cosmological constant. |
| 1999  | Measurements of the cosmic microwave background radiation most notably by the BOOMERanG experiment (Balloon Observations Of Millimetric Extragalactic Radiation and Geophysics) (Mauskopf et al., 1999, Melchiorri et al., 1999, de Bernardis et al., 2000) provide evidence for oscillations (peaks) in the anisotropy angular spectrum as expected in the standard model of cosmological structure formation. These results indicate that the geometry of the universe is flat. Together with large scale structure data, this provides complementary evidence for a non-zero cosmological constant. |

| | |
|---|---|
| 2003 | NASA's Wilkinson Microwave Anisotropy Probe (WMAP) satellite takes more detailed pictures of the cosmic microwave background radiation than were obtained by the BOOMERanG experiment. The images confirm the universe is $13.73\pm0.12$ billion years old (within one percent error) and that the Lambda-CDM model and the inflationary theory of the universe are correct. |
| 2003 | An apparent periodicity in the cosmic microwave background leads to the suggestion, by Jean-Pierre Luminet of the Observatoire de Paris and colleagues, that the shape of the universe is a finite dodecahedron, attached to itself by each pair of opposite faces to form a Poincare sphere. During the following year, astronomers search for more evidence to support this hypothesis but find none. |
| 2006 | The three-year WMAP results are released, confirming previous WMAP data analysis, correcting several points, and additionally including polarization data. |

## References

Bunch, Bryan, and Alexander Hellemans, *"The History of Science and Technology: A Browser's Guide to the Great Discoveries, Inventions, and the People Who Made Them from the Dawn of Time to Today."* ISBN 0-618-22123-9.

P. Mauskopf et al., astro-ph/9911444, Astrophys.J. 536 (2000) l59-L62.

A. Melchiorri et al., astro-ph/9911445, Astrophys.J. 536 (2000) L63-L66.

P. de Bernardis et al., astro-ph/0004404, Nature **404** (2000) 955-959.

Retrieved from "http://en.wikipedia.org/wiki/Timeline_of_ cosmology"

# Timeline of Artificial Satellites and Space Probes

Retrieved from Wikipedia—the on-line encyclopedia
http://en.wikipedia.org/wiki/Timeline_of_artificial_satellites_an
d_space_probes

Currently there are over 2,200 man-made satellites circling the earth. The following **Timeline of Artificial Satellites and Space Probes** includes unmanned spacecraft including technology demonstrators, observatories, lunar probes, and interplanetary probes. First satellites from each country are included. Not included are Earth science satellites, commercial satellites, and manned missions.

**Key**: Year - Origin - Target - Status - Description

## 1950s

1957 -  Soviet Union - Earth - Success - *Sputnik 1* is launched, the first Earth orbiting satellite

1957 -  Soviet Union - Earth - Partial Success - Sputnik 2 is launched, the first Earth orbiting satellite with an animal (Laika)

1958 -  USA - Earth - Success - Explorer 1

1958 -  USA - Earth - Failure - Explorer 2

1958 -  USA - Earth - Success - Vanguard 1 is the oldest satellite still orbiting Earth (as of June 2009).

1958 -  USA - Earth - Success - Explorer 3 is the first satellite to carry a tape recorder, allowing delayed transmission of data to ground stations.

1958 -  USA - Earth - Success - Explorer 4 elliptical orbiter

1958 -  USA - Earth - Failure - Explorer 5

1958 -  USA - Earth - Failure - Beacon 1

1958 -  USA - Moon - Failure - Pioneer 1 orbiter

1958 -  USA - Moon - Failure - Pioneer 3 flyby

1958 - USA - Earth - Success - Project_SCORE, the first communications satellite, broadcasts President's Christmas message.

1959 - USA - Earth - Success - Explorer 6 provides the first pictures of Earth from orbit

1959 - USA - Earth - Success - Explorer 7

1959 - Soviet Union - Moon - Partial Success - Luna 1 The lunar impactor is launched but misses target and enters heliocentric orbit. It discovered solar wind.

1959 - USA - Moon - Partial success - Pioneer 4 flyby

1959 - Soviet Union - Moon - Success - Luna 2 Impactor launched; it is the first spacecraft to impact onto the surface of the moon.

1959 - Soviet Union - Moon - Success - Luna 3 Flyby launched; it returns the first image of the Moon's hidden side.

## 1960s

1960 - USA - Sun - Success -Pioneer 5 solar monitor

1960 - USA - Earth - Success - TIROS 1 weather satellite

1960 - Soviet Union - Mars - Failure - Mars 1960A probe

1960 - Soviet Union - Mars - Failure - Mars 1960B probe

1960 - USA - Earth - Failure - Courier 1A communications

1960 - USA - Earth - Success - Courier 1B communications

1961 - Soviet Union - Venus - Failure - 1VA (proto-Venera) flyby

1961 - Soviet Union - Venus - Failure - Venera 1 flyby

1961 - USA - Earth - Success - OSCAR1 is the first amateur satellite

1962 - USA - Venus - Success - Mariner 2 launches and becomes the first satellite to return data about Venus.

1962 - USA - Earth - Success - Telstar 1 is launched.

1962 - UK - Earth - Success - Ariel 1 launches on a US rocket, is the first UK satellite, and is the first satellite operated by a country other than the United States or Soviet Union.

1962 - Canada - Earth - Success - Alouette 1 is launches as the first Canadian satellite and the first satellite built by a country other than the United States or Soviet Union.

1962 - USA - Moon - Failure - Ranger 3 photographic mission

1962 - USA - Moon - Partial Failure - Ranger 4 photographic mission (impacted lunar surface)

1962 - USA - Moon - Partial Failure - Ranger 5 photographic mission (became flyby)

1962 - Soviet Union - Mars - Failure - Mars 1962A flyby

1962 - Soviet Union - Mars - Failure - Mars 1 flyby

1962 - Soviet Union - Mars - Failure - Mars 1962B lander

1963 - USA - Earth - Failure - Syncom 1 is launched.

1963 - USA - Earth - Success - Syncom 2 is launched and makes the first geosynchronous orbit.

1963 - Soviet Union - Moon - Partial Failure - Luna 4 lander (became probe)

1964 - USA - Earth - Success - Syncom 3 is launched and makes the first geostationary orbit.

1964 - Soviet Union - Venus - Failure - Zond 1 flyby

1964 - USA - Moon - Failure - Ranger 6 photographic mission

1962 - UK - Earth - Success - Ariel 2

1964 - USA - Moon - Success - Ranger 7 photographic mission

1964 - USA - Mars - Failure - Mariner 3 flyby

1964 - USA - Mars - Success - Mariner 4 flyby, the first successful Mars mission

1964 - Soviet Union - Mars - Failure - Zond 2 flyby

1964 - Italy - Earth - Success - San Marco 1 is launched aboard a U.S. Scout from the base of Wallops Island and is the first Italian satellite

1965 - USA - Sun - Success - Pioneer 6 solar probe

1965 - Soviet Union - Venus - Failure - Venera 2 flyby

1965 - Soviet Union - Venus - Failure - Venera 3 atmospheric probe

1965 - USA - Moon - Success - Ranger 8 photographic mission

1965 - USA - Moon - Success - Ranger 9 photographic mission

1965 - Canada - Earth - Success - Alouette 2 is launched aboard a U.S. rocket.

1965 - Soviet Union - Moon - Failure - Luna 5 lander

1965 - Soviet Union - Moon - Failure - Luna 6 lander
1965 - Soviet Union - Moon - Success - Zond 3 flyby
1965 - Soviet Union - Moon - Failure - Luna 7 lander
1965 - France - Satellite - Success - Astérix satellite is launched in French Diamant A rocket and is the first French satellite.
1965 - Soviet Union - Moon - Failure - Luna 8 lander
1965 - USA - Mars - Success - Mariner 4 sends the first clear pictures of Mars.
1966 - USA - Sun - Success - Pioneer 7 solar probe
1966 - Soviet Union - Moon - Success - Luna 9 lander returns the first photographs from the surface of the Moon.
1966 - Soviet Union - Moon - Success - Luna 10 becomes the first spacecraft to orbit the Moon.
1966 - USA - Moon - Success - Surveyor 1 lander
1966 - USA - Moon - Success - Lunar Orbiter 1 orbiter
1966 - Soviet Union - Moon - Success - Luna 11 orbiter
1966 - USA - Moon - Failure - Surveyor 2
1966 - Soviet Union - Moon - Success - Luna 12 orbiter
1966 - USA - Moon - Success - Lunar Orbiter 2 orbiter
1966 - Soviet Union - Moon - Success - Luna 13 lander
1967 - Australia - Earth - Success - WRESAT is launched from Woomera on a U.S. Redstone rocket and is the first Australian satellite
1967 - USA - Sun - Success - Pioneer 8 solar probe
1967 - Soviet Union - Venus - Success - Venera 4 sends the first data from below the clouds of Venus
1967 - USA - Venus - Success - Mariner 5 flyby
1967 - USA - Moon - Success - Lunar Orbiter 3 orbiter
1967 - USA - Moon - Success - Surveyor 2 lander
1967 - USA - Moon - Success - Lunar Orbiter 4 orbiter
1967 - USA - Moon - Failure - Surveyor 3 lander
1967 - UK - Earth - Success - Ariel 3
1967 - USA - Moon - Success - Explorer 35 orbiter
1967 - USA - Moon - Success - Lunar Orbiter 5 orbiter
1967 - USA - Moon - Success - Surveyor 5 lander
1967 - USA - Moon - Success - Surveyor 6 lander, also took off from the Moon's surface

1967 - USA - Success - The OSO-3 gamma-ray satellite discovers gamma-ray emission from the plane of the Milky Way

1968 - USA - Sun - Success - Pioneer 9 solar probe

1968 - USA - Moon - Success - Surveyor 7 lander

1968 - Soviet Union - Moon - Success - Luna 14 orbiter

1968 - Soviet Union - Moon - Success - Zond 5 flyby

1968 - Soviet Union - Moon - Success - Zond 6 flyby

1969 - Soviet Union - Venus - Success - Venera 5 atmospheric probe

1969 - Soviet Union - Venus - Success - Venera 6 atmospheric probe

1969 - Soviet Union - Moon - Failure - Luna 15 lander

1969 - Soviet Union - Moon - Success - Zond 7 flyby

1969 - USA - Mars - Success - Mariner 6 flyby

1969 - USA - Mars - Success - Mariner 7 flyby

## 1970s

1970 - Japan - Earth - Success - Osumi is the first Japanese satellite.

1970 - Soviet Union - Venus - Success - Venera 7 makes the first successful landing of a spacecraft on another planet.

1970 - Soviet Union - Moon - Success - Luna 16 lander is the first automated return of samples from the Moon.

1970 - Soviet Union - Moon - Success - Zond 8 flyby

1970 - Soviet Union - Moon - Success - Luna 17/Lunokhod 1 lander/rover is the first automated surface exploration of the Moon.

1970 - USA - Success - Launch of Uhuru, the first dedicated X-ray satellite

1970 - China - Success - Launch of Dong Fang Hong I, the first Chinese satellite

1971 - Soviet Union - Moon - Failure - Luna 18 lander

1971 - Soviet Union - Moon - Success - Luna 19 orbiter

1971 - USA - Mars - Failure - Mariner 8 flyby

1971 - Soviet Union - Mars - Failure - Cosmos 419 probe

1971 - Soviet Union - Mars - Partial Failure - Mars 2 orbiter and lander creates the first human artifact on Mars.

1971 - Soviet Union - Mars - Partial Success - Mars 3 orbiter and lander makes first successful landing on Mars

1971 - USA - Mars - Success - Mariner 9 orbiter takes first pictures of Mars' moons (Phobos and Deimos).

1971 - UK - Earth - Success - Prospero X-3 satellite is the first and only satellite launched by Britain using a British rocket.

1971 - UK - Earth - Success - Ariel 4

1972 - Soviet Union - Venus - Success - Venera 8 lander

1972 - Soviet Union - Moon - Success - Luna 20 lander

1972 - USA - Success - Launch of the Copernicus ultraviolet satellite

1972 - USA - Sun - Success - Explorer 49 solar probe

1973 - USA - Venus/Mercury - Success - Mariner 10 launched, it passes by and photographs Mercury; also is the first dual planet probe.

1973 - Soviet Union - Moon - Success - Luna 21/Lunokhod 2 lander/rover

1973 - Soviet Union - Mars - Failure - Mars 4 orbiter

1973 - Soviet Union - Mars - Success - Mars 5 orbiter

1973 - Soviet Union - Mars - Failure - Mars 6 orbiter and lander

1973 - Soviet Union - Mars - Failure - Mars 7 orbiter and lander

1974 - West Germany - Sun - Success - Helios 1 solar probe

1974 - Soviet Union - Moon - Success - Luna 22 orbiter

1974 - Soviet Union - Moon - Failure - Luna 23 probe

1974 - UK - Earth - Success - Launch of the Ariel 5 X-ray satellite

1975 - Soviet Union - Venus - Success - Venera 9 returns the first pictures of the surface of Venus.

1975 - Soviet Union - Venus - Success - Venera 10 orbiter and lander

1975 - USA - Mars - Partial Success - Viking 1 orbiter and lander; lands on Mars

1975 - USA - Mars - Success - Viking 2 orbiter and lander; lands on Mars 1976

1975 - India - Earth - Success - Aryabhata India, launched by USSR

1975 - India - Launches first Satellite Launch Vehicle

1976 - West Germany - Sun - Success - Helios 2 solar probe

1976 - Soviet Union - Moon - Success - Luna 24 lander

1976 - USA - Earth - Success - Hermes Communications Technology Satellite serves as the prototype for testing direct broadcast TV.

1976 - USA - Success - The Vela and ANS X-ray satellites discover X-ray bursts.

1976 - USA - Success - The OSO-8 X-ray satellite shows X-ray bursts have blackbody spectra.

1977 - USA - Success - Launch of the HEAO-1 X-ray satellite

1978 - USA - Venus - Success - Pioneer Venus 1 orbiter

1978 - USA - Venus - Success - Pioneer Venus 2 atmospheric probe

1978 - Soviet Union - Venus - Partial Success - Venera 11 flyby and lander

1978 - Soviet Union - Venus - Success - Venera 12 flyby and lander

1978 - USA - Success - Launch of the International Ultraviolet Explorer satellite

1978 - USA - Success - Launch of the Einstein X-ray satellite (HEAO-2) is the first X-ray photographs of astronomical objects

1979 - USA - Success - Launch of the Hakucho X-ray satellite

1979 - UK - Earth - Success - Launch of the Ariel 6 cosmic-ray and X-ray satellite

1979 - USA - Jupiter - Success - Voyager 1 and Voyager 2 send back images of Jupiter and its system

1979 - India - Earth - Success - Bhaskara-1 India, launched by ISRO (First Indian low orbit Earth Observation Satellite)

## 1980s

1980 - USA - Sun - Failure- Solar Maximum Mission solar probe succeeds after being repaired in Earth orbit

1981 - India - Earth - Success - Bhaskara-2 India, launched by ISRO

1981 - Soviet Union - Venus - Success - Venera 13 launches and returns the first color pictures of the surface of Venus.

1981 - Soviet Union - Venus - Success - Venera 14 flyby and lander

1981 - Bulgaria - Earth - Success - Bulgaria 1300 is a polar research mission launched by the Soviet Union.

1983 - Soviet Union - Venus - Success - Venera 15 orbiter

1983 - Soviet Union - Venus - Success - Venera 16 orbiter

1983 - USA - Success - Launch of the EXOSAT X-ray satellite

1983 - USA - Success - Launch of the Tenma X-ray satellite (ASTRO-B)

1983 - USA - Success - Launch of the IRAS satellite

1984 - Soviet Union - Venus/Halley's Comet - Success - Vega 1 flyby, atmospheric probe and lander

1984 - Soviet Union - Venus/Halley's Comet - Success - Vega 2 flyby, atmospheric probe and lander

1986 - Europe - Halley's Comet - Success - Giotto flyby

1987 - USA - Success - Launch of the Ginga X-ray satellite (ASTRO-C)

1988 - Soviet Union - Mars - Failure - Phobos 1 orbiter and lander

1988 - Soviet Union - Mars - Partial Failure - Phobos 2 flyby and lander

1989 - USA - Venus - Success - Magellan orbiter launches and maps 99% of the surface of Venus (300 m resolution)

1989 - USA - Venus/Earth/Moon/Gaspra/Ida/Jupiter - Success - Galileo flyby, orbiter and atmospheric probe

1989 - USA - Neptune - Success - Voyager 2 sends back images of Neptune and its system.

1989 - USA - Success - Launch of the Granat gamma-ray and X-ray satellite

1989 - Europe - Success - Launch of the Hipparcos satellite
1989 - USA - Success - Launch of the COBE satellite

## 1990s

1990 - USA - Sun - Success - Ulysses solar flyby
1990 - Japan - Moon - - MUSES-A probe is the first non-United States or USSR probe to reach the Moon
1990 - USA/ Europe - Success - Launch of the Hubble Space Telescope
1990 - Germany - Success - Launch of the ROSAT X-ray satellite is the first imaging X-ray sky survey.
1991 - Japan - Sun - Success - Yohkoh solar probe
1991 - USA - Success - Launch of the Compton Gamma-Ray Observatory satellite
1992 - USA - Mars - Failure - Mars Observer orbiter
1993 - Japan - Success - Launch of the ASCA (ASTRO-D) X-ray satellite
1994 - USA - Moon - Success - Clementine orbiter maps the surface of the Moon (resolution 125-150m) and allows the first accurate relief map of the Moon to be generated.
1995 - USA - Sun - Success - SOHO solar probe
1996 - USA - Mars - Mars Global Surveyor orbiter
1996 - USA - Mars - Success - Mars Pathfinder/Sojourner lander/rover is the first automated surface exploration another planet.
1996 - Russia - Mars - Failure - Mars 96 orbiter and lander
1997 - USA/Europe - Success - Saturn and Titan - Cassini-Huygens arrives in orbit on July 1, 2004, and lands on Titan January 14, 2005.
1998 - North Korea - Unknown - Claimed launch of Kwangmyongsong by North Korea though no independent source is able to verify its existence
1998 - USA - Moon - Success - Lunar Prospector orbiter
1998 - Japan - Mars - Failure - Nozomi (Planet B) orbiter, the first Japanese spacecraft to reach another planet
1998 - USA - Mars - Failure - Mars Climate Orbiter
1999 - USA - Mars - Failure - Mars Polar Lander

1999 - USA - Mars - Failure - Deep Space 2 (DS2) penetrators

1999 - USA - Earth - Success - Launch of the Chandra X-ray Observatory

1999 - Europe - Earth - Success - Launch of the X-Ray Multi-Mirror Mission, XMM-Newton

## 2000s

2001 - USA - Sun - Partial Success - Genesis solar wind sample returns; crash-lands on return.

2001 - USA - Success - Wilkinson Microwave Anisotropy Probe (WMAP) performs cosmological observations.

2001 - USA - Mars - Success - Mars Odyssey

2003 - Canada - Earth - Success - MOST, the smallest space telescope in orbit

2003 - USA - Comet Encke - Failure - CONTOUR is launched but lost during early trajectory insertion.

2003 - Europe - Moon - Success - Smart 1 orbiter

2003 - Europe - Mars - Partial Success - Mars Express orbiter (successfully reached orbit) and failed lander, the Beagle 2

2003 - USA - Mars - Success - Mars Exploration Rovers - successful launches, Spirit successfully lands, Opportunity successfully lands

2003 - Japan - 25143 Itokawa - Hayabusa - sample returns - arrives 2010

2004 - Europe - Comet 67P - Rosetta space probe launches - yet to arrive

2004 - USA - Mercury - MESSENGER orbiter - launches - yet to arrive

2004 - USA - Success - Launch of the Swift Gamma ray burst observatory.

2005 - Iran - Earth - Sinah-1 - launched, first Iranian-built satellite

2005 - USA - Comet Tempel 1 - Deep Impact - successful comet impact

2005 - USA - Mars - Mars Reconnaissance Orbiter - in orbit

2005 - Europe - Venus - Venus Express - in orbit

2006 - USA - Pluto - New Horizons - launches - yet to arrive

2006 - France/ESA - Earth - COROT launches with telescope to search for extrasolar planets.

2007 - USA - Mars - Success - Phoenix launches and successfully lands in 2008

2007 - Japan - Moon - SELENE orbiter and lander - in lunar orbit since October 3, 2007

2007 - USA - Vesta/Ceres- Dawn - launches - yet to arrive

2007 - China - Moon - Chang'e-I - success - lunar orbiter

2009 - Iran - Earth - Omid - launched by Iranian made launcher Safir, first Iranian-launched satellite

2009 - India - Earth - Success - RISAT-2, developed by Israel Aerospace Industries, launched by ISRO, India

2009 - India - Moon - Success - Chandrayaan-1, developed and launched by ISRO, India

## 2010s

2010 - Japan - Venus - Akatsuki orbiter - failed orbital insertion

2010 - Japan - Venus IKAROS - first solar-sail spacecraft launches

2010 - China - Moon - Chang'e-2 - success - lunar orbiter/impactor

2011 - USA - Jupiter - Juno - launched and *en route*

Evolution to Humans. Peabody Museum, Yale University

# CHAPTER 2

## Evolution: Life

Earth is the only planet in the universe known at this time to be inhabited with life. How and when did life on Earth get to be the way it is today? Imagine a world without bees, butterflies, and flowering plants. That was Earth 125 million years ago. Turn back the clock 400 million years, and there were no trees. At 450 million years in the past, even the earliest insect had not yet developed. And looking back 500 million years, the land was devoid of life; however, at that time life flourished in a profusion of strange forms in the oceans.

Evolution is the most remarkable force in the history of Earth, the organizing principle throughout the biological sciences, and the most important mechanism scientists use to understand the varieties of life on our planet. Evolution of the various life forms required appropriate environments. For most of its first 1 billion years Earth did not have an environment conducive to life. It was a planet in turmoil bombarded by meteors and laden with volcanic activity, but the forces of nature brought change and we exist at a time when the environment supports life. It is a very special environment and we are extremely lucky to be the benefactors of such an environment.

Life on Earth emerged 3.8 billion years ago in its first microscopic forms. This was about ten billion years after the Big

Bang, about 5 billion years after the formation of the first stars, and about 750 million years after the earth formed. Why did it take so long for life to emerge? In order to provide the chemical abundances required for life, it is estimated that three generations of stars were required. It is only through nucleosynthesis in stellar interiors that the heavier elements can be created. At the death of stars this material is regurgitated to form the matter for a new generation of stars. The lifetime of a star depends on its total mass and can vary from several millions of years for a very massive star to tens of billions of years for lower mass stars. At any rate, it took about 10 billion years of stellar evolution to produce the elements needed for life to evolve. Our bodies consist of the elements from stardust.

Only about a dozen different minerals, including diamonds and graphite, in dust grains pre-date our solar system. Another fifty or so formed as the sun ignited. On Earth, volcanoes emitted basalt and plate tectonics made ores of copper, lead, and zinc. The minerals were players in the epic story of exploding stars and planetary formation and the triggering of plate tectonics. And then life played a key role. By introducing oxygen into the atmosphere, photosynthesis made possible new kinds of minerals such as turquoise, azurite, and malachite. Mosses and algae climbed onto land, breaking down rock and making clay, which made bigger plants possible, which made deeper soil, and so on. Today there are about 4,400 known minerals, more than two-thirds of which came into being only because of the way life changed the planet. Some of them were created exclusively by living organisms.

There is a symbiotic relationship between minerals and life that has existed through time that has led to increasing complexity. It is this complexity around hydrothermal vents in the ocean, with gushing hot water mixing with cold water near rocks and ore deposits, which provided an environment where amino acids could congregate. It is this environment that makes it such a good candidate to be the cradle of life on Earth. The origin of life used rocks, it used water, it used atmosphere. Once life got a foothold, the fact that the environment is so variable drives evolution. Minerals evolved; life arose and diversified; and then along came trilobites, whales, and primates.

The region around a star that can support life on a planet is known as the habitable zone. The inner and outer radii of this zone vary with the luminosity of the star, as does the time interval during which the zone will survive. Stars more massive than our sun have a larger habitable zone but have a shorter time interval during which life could evolve. Stars in the intermediate mass range such as our sun seem to possess the optimal conditions for Earth-like life to develop. The size of Earth is well suited to life as we know it. On a much larger planet, the gravitational pull on the atmosphere would be so great that the atmosphere would be too dense to admit sunlight, which is a fundamental source of energy for life. A much smaller planet would lack sufficient gravitational attraction to retain an atmosphere with life-giving oxygen.

Between 4.1 billion and 3.8 billion years ago, Earth was pummeled by comets and cold meteorites—both of which carry water, and at that point much of Earth's water was in place setting the stage for the earliest forms of microbial life about 3.6 billion years ago. In addition, Earth's temperatures are such that most of its free water is liquid, the form that seems to be essential for life. As stated in Chapter 1, by the end of 2011, the number of potential planets identified by the Kepler satellite in its first sixteen months of operation was up to 2326. It has also confirmed the discovery of its first planet in a star's habitable zone—the "Goldilocks" zone where liquid water could exist. The Kepler satellite is expected to examine over 156,000 stars between 2010 and 2013 in a very small portion (1/400) of the Milky Way galaxy.

Considering there are hundreds of billions of galaxies in our universe, with most having hundreds of billions of stars, it is statistically probable that there are many planets that could harbor some forms of life, probably even Earth-like life. The "Kepler 11" solar system has six planets in orbit around its star. One recently found planet known as Gliese 581g lies in an orbit around a red dwarf star and looks to be in a habitable zone. It appears to be tidally locked to its star, with one side perpetually facing its star and the other side perpetually dark. The part facing its star must be extremely hot and the part facing away must be extremely cold. However, there could well be a livable zone along the line between shadow and light that's not too hot and not too cold—a Goldilocks zone wherein there could be liquid water and be just right for life.

A recently found planet, HD85512b, is even more likely to be able to harbor life than Gliese 581g. It is thirty-six light years away in the southern sky in the constellation Vela and has a mass 3.5 times that of the Earth. It is one of fifty newly found planets, announced in September 2011, of which sixteen have the right mass to be rock instead of gas. Several astrophysicists have predicted that alien life will be discovered by 2050, and some have predicted by as early as 2025 (most likely not intelligent life).

There are fundamental laws that apply to the entire universe. Because those fundamental laws allowed intelligent life to develop on Earth, they ought to engender intelligent life elsewhere, too. There's a good chance that there's life right here in our galaxy. With so many habitable planets, it's hard to imagine that there wouldn't be. And, at some point we will probably discover it.

So, just what is life? Life is a characteristic that distinguishes objects that have signaling and self-sustaining processes from those that do not. Life is the condition that distinguishes active organisms from inorganic matter. Living organisms undergo metabolism, regulate their internal environment to maintain a stable constant condition, possess a capacity to grow, respond to stimuli, reproduce, and, through natural selection, adapt to their environment in successive generations. On Earth plants, animals, fungi, protists, archaea, and bacteria are all carbon- and water-based cellular forms with complex organization and heritable genetic information which are considered forms of life. Viruses, on the other hand, are not usually considered forms of life, even though they possess genes, evolve by natural selection, and replicate by creating multiple copies of themselves through self-assembly, they do not metabolize and they require host cells to reproduce. The self-assembly of viruses within host cells does, however, have implications for the study of the origin of life, as it supports the hypothesis that life could have started as self-assembling organic molecules.

The earliest life forms probably resulted from self-reproducing ribonucleic acid (RNA) molecules. The replication of these organisms required resources like energy, space, and smaller building blocks, which soon become limited, resulting in competition, wherein natural selection favored those molecules which were more efficient at replication. Deoxyribonucleic acid (DNA) molecules then evolved and took over as the main replicators and these archaic genomes soon developed inside enclosed membranes which provided a stable physical and chemical environment conducive to their replication.

In 1953 a graduate student, Stanley Miller, working on his doctoral thesis at the University of Chicago, performed an experiment that showed how amino acids, the building blocks of proteins needed for life, could easily be generated from the simple chemicals assumed to have been present on primitive Earth. The origin of the experiment lay in the work of his advisor at the university, geochemist Harold Urey, who argued in 1951 that the atmosphere of early Earth would have consisted of water vapor, ammonia, and methane, with no oxygen. Miller set up a flask of water, to represent the oceans, connected to a flask of gases through which he passed electrical discharges to represent lightning. After just two days, there were signs that glycine, a simple amino acid, had been created, and by the end of the week several more of life's essential building blocks had turned up in the seething mixture. After two weeks of sparks and bubbles, the fluid changed in color. When Miller analyzed the resulting brew, he found at least two amino acids had been formed. Since then the experiment has been repeated many times combining different atmospheres and sources of energy. Most of the amino acid forms have been created by these experiments. However, the big step from amino acids to life forms has not been accomplished yet in the lab.

Another researcher, George Cody, a senior scientist at the Carnegie Institution of Washington, has been investigating how building blocks for life might have managed to survive the immense heat of early Earth. He and other scientist think they have found the answer: the organics were locked in stable chains formed from formaldehyde, an ironic finding considering that formaldehyde ended up being poisonous to the very life it may have made possible. Formaldehyde is very interesting, very reactive. It can even react with itself and form complex polymers. Formaldehyde also is plentiful in molecular clouds in space, meaning ample quantities would have been around for incorporation into the solar system's population. Two chains of evidence support this theory. First, organic solids have been found in meteorites and in comets. A sample from NASA's Stardust comet mission gave Cody and colleagues a sign they were on the right path. "It was about the most chemically complex material I had ever seen in my life," Cody said. Scientists then turned to lab work to reproduce the type of organic matter found in carbonaceous chondrites, a type of organic-rich meteorite, from formaldehyde. They found their formaldehyde-synthesized material was similar to what has been found in carbonaceous chondrites and from the Wild 2 comet, which was sampled by NASA's Stardust probe. The experiments also showed the organics would survive temperatures of up to 1,400 Centigrade (2,552 degrees Fahrenheit). Formaldehyde is almost unique in its tendency to hang out—and hang on—as the solar system got hotter and dryer. Also buttressing the team's findings is a related study showing that comets may be much more watery than previously thought. If liquid water environments were common, then there are a lot more places to produce pre-biotic material.

On September 28, 1969, an asteroid fell in Murchison, Australia. Analysis of this space rock revealed that it contained graphite, amino acids, and almost 250 different hydrocarbons, and most important, the five nitrogenized bases of DNA: adeninc, guanine, cytosine, thymine, and uracil. This means the asteroid experienced extensive alteration by water-rich fluids on its parent body before falling to Earth. This still does not tell us that life forms existed on the parent body, but it does raise the possibility.

We don't know for sure if primitive life forms could have formed naturally here on Earth, but we do know that once they did occur, from whatever source, they then evolved. We don't know if individual life forms of the same type began separately or if many of the same type formed in the same timeframe in a particular environment. And, we don't know if perhaps several different life forms started their existence independently at different times in different environments. We do know, however, that during the onset of life, Earth was a very volatile place and there were different environments in which primitive life could have gotten a foothold. For example, on the Pacific Ocean floor there are volcanic geysers—chimneys of rock from which boiling water emerges. A type of bacteria named arqueobacteria has installed itself there in temperatures of up to 350 degrees Celsius. These bacteria grow in hostile conditions similar to those that the primitive atmosphere presented and they don't consume oxygen.

Bob Hazen, a researcher at the Carnegie lab, has demonstrated that the basic molecules for life are able to form in many places: near hydrothermal vents, volcanoes, and even on meteorites. Drilling studies show that microbes live in every possible subterranean environment, from buried desert sands to mile-deep Antarctic ice, to pristine rock in the bowels of gold mines. Possibly, the story of life could have started underground, where water and chemically unstable rocks provided the chemical energy to power the emergence of life.

A geophysicist, Louis Lerma, upholds that bubbles on the surface of the primitive oceans could have contained a solution similar to that in Stanley Miller's experiment playing a similar role. The turbulence of whitecaps and crashing waves produced a continuous fine mist in which organic molecules may have reacted with water and air to produce cell-like structures that were the precursors to life. Whether forming perhaps in ocean surface bubbles, or at the bottom of the ocean, or coming from outer space, or from all of these sources, we don't know for sure. We do know for certain though that some of the first organic compounds went through a metamorphosis that made them capable of storing genetic information and, at the same time, carry out catalytical reactions, and that probably RNA molecules formed from them.

Professor Graham Cairns-Smith, from the University of Glasgow, speculates that before the first life forms on Earth existed, it is possible that a world of clay organisms was present. Crystals in clay posses the ability of replicating themselves, growing and, in a certain way evolve through natural selection. This is due to the fact that these crystals are not perfect and contain small defects that can be repeated. In this way, crystals that can reproduce better than others or which are more resistant than their counterparts could exist. At some time along the way this system of loamy clay could have come to the point where it included in its structure organic molecules, specifically RNA that through the passage of time could have gained control of the evolutionary process. It is not known how such organic matter could have come together to originate the first cells, but certainly evolution from crystals in clay is one possibility for the first cells.

Another scenario is that of flat life, wherein the very first self-replicating entity was a thin layer of chemical reactants that grew on mineral surfaces. This flat life spread from mineral grain to mineral grain as a coating of organic molecules too thin to see. Extensive colonies of flat life might survive even today in deeper parts of Earth's crust.

A recent report in *Science Daily* (October 26, 2011) is that many of the organic molecules that make up life on Earth have also been found in space. By analyzing spectra of star dust formed in exploding stars called novae, Professor Sun Kwok and Dr. Yong Zhang of The University of Hong Kong have shown that these stars are making complex organic compounds on extremely short time scales of weeks. Not only are these stars producing complex organic matter, they are also ejecting it into the general interstellar space. Whether these organic compounds played any role in the development of life on Earth remains an open question.

Most of life's history involved the biochemical evolution of single-celled microorganisms. Fossilized microbes have been found in rocks 3.5 billion years old. However, multi-celled fossils have only been identified in rocks younger than 1 billion years. For the first 85% of the past 3.8 billion years, only single-celled organisms existed. The oldest microbial communities often constructed layered mound-shaped deposits called stromatolites, whose structures suggest that those organisms sought light and were therefore photosynthetic. These early stromatolites grew along seacoasts and endured harsh sunlight as well as episodic wetting and drying by tides. Stromatolites still exist in several spots throughout the world. Today they can be found mostly along the coastlines of Western Australia and the Bahamas. They use carbon dioxide (formed primarily by volcanic activity) as a carbon source and have released enormous amounts of oxygen into Earth's atmosphere. In so doing they paved the way for aerobic-based life to emerge and diversify.

**Stromatolites**

Retrieved from:
http://paleontology.edwardtbabinski.us/vendian/stromatolites.jpg

Credit: Edward T. Babinski. Image based on *Kingfisher Illustrated Dinosaur Encyclopedia*, David Burnie, 2001.

The Earth has proven to be an ideal environment for complex life to evolve. From Everest's peak to the floor of the Mariana Trench, creatures of one kind or another inhabit virtually every square inch of the planetary surface. Earth's incubator has allowed microorganisms, such as bacteria and viruses, to become a diversity of life. Microbes also have proven that they can survive in space. A bacterium called Deinococcus radiodarans can live through radiation so intense the glass of a Pyrex beaker in which they reside will cook to a discolored fragile condition. These critters can withstand radiation about 1,000 times that which would kill humans. A small number will survive three million rads. 1,000 rads will kill a human in one to two weeks. These guys are super bugs and certainly are candidates for space travel.

When the first astronauts landed on the moon in 1969, they retrieved a piece of an unmanned moon vehicle of the Surveyor series. Bacteria found on the retrieved part, exposed to the moon's environment for more than seven years, were still alive. There was an experiment on board the space station that exposed microbes to space. The shuttle *Challenger*'s crew was supposed to retrieve this experiment and return it to researchers on Earth. *Challenger* exploded on lift off and the microbe experiment remained exposed to a space environment for more than three years. Subsequent retrieval and examination of the experiment found the bacteria had survived by creating a cocoon around some members of their colony.

There is evidence that microbes can remain dormant indefinitely. About 30 million years ago a bee was killed by resin that over time turned into amber, which served as its tomb until now. Within the bee's belly a microbiologist, Dr. Raul Cano, a professor at the Biological Sciences Department at California Polytechnic State University in San Luis Obispo, found more than two thousand species of bacteria and yeast that had survived those millions of years of entombment. When environmental conditions in a pristine laboratory reached life support levels, these critters came alive!

Almost every global influenza outbreak involves microbes that are unique to that particular outbreak. The influenza pandemic of 1918–19 killed from 20 to 30 million people across every inhabited continent. Physicians were helpless as the origin of this influenza variant was not precisely known. The accepted thought was that the virus originated in China where a rare genetic shift took place to change the virus.

Immediately after Halley's Comet visited the solar system in April 1910, Earth's orbit took the planet directly through the comet's plume. Water latent dust and other debris entered Earth's upper atmosphere. Some researchers believe the influenza virus that caused the 1918 outbreak could have arrived via Halley's Comet. Circumstantial evidence leads one to believe the seeds of life could have possibly been left in the dust debris left by a passing comet.

The aforementioned evidence drives the search for life on Mars and elsewhere in space. The Viking Landers of the 1970s were designed to search for life on the surface of Mars. Several experiments were on board that involved the collection of soil, applying nutrients to that soil sample, and analyzing waste that could have been generated by microbes. The first experiment used a radiation marker that gave a positive indication something alive had processed the soil sample. Further experiments could not verify these results, so NASA retracted their findings that life had been discovered on Mars. Later, experiments were conducted on Earth using twin Viking instruments that analyzed soil enriched with microbes and the devices failed.

Somewhere between 3.9 and 2.5 billion years ago, a group of organisms named prokaryotes, which lack a cell nucleus, emerged on Earth. Most are unicellular, but a few have multi-cellular stages in their life cycles. Life's first major evolutionary transition was the leap from basic prokaryotic to more complex eukaryotic cells around 2.1 billion years ago. These cells contain membrane-bound organelles with diverse functions, and derived from prokaryotes.

Around 1.2 billion years ago, sexual reproduction first appeared, increasing the rate of evolution. Simple multi-cellular organisms evolved, mostly consisting of cell colonies of limited complexity. Between 580 and 542 million years ago ediacaran biota appeared. They represent the first large, complex multi-cellular organisms. Between 580 and 540 million years ago the accumulation of atmospheric oxygen allowed for the formation of an ozone layer. The ozone layer blocks ultraviolet radiation, and thus permitted the colonization of the land. Between 580 and 500 million years ago most modern phyla of animals begin to appear in the fossil record during the Cambrian explosion. Around 560 million years ago the earliest fungi began to appear in the fossil records.

The fossil record shows that starting at about 535 million years ago there was major diversification of living things in the oceans. The first known signs of life on land date to about 530 million years ago. About 505 million years ago a form of jawless fish appeared. These fish were the first vertebrates. Jawed fish evolved from jawless fish about 480 million years ago, their jaws evolving from the first of their gill arched. The evolution or predators triggered an evolutionary response—mineralized skeletons as a defense. About 450 million years ago land arthropods (millipedes) evolved. The first primitive land plants evolved from green algae 434 million years ago.

The iconic image of evolution is a fish emerging onto land. This transition might not have happened without shade provided by the newly developing forests, whose protective canopy gave the first "fishapods" protection from the sun. The canopies provided by early vegetation gave vertebrates new opportunities to get out of the water and start moving around on land. All four-limbed vertebrates (tetrapods) owe their evolutionary origins to lobe-finned fish that started this transition about 380 million years ago. They were likely the first vertebrates to come onto land.

By 363 million years ago insects roamed the land, sharks ruled the oceans, and vegetation covered the land. The first crabs and ferns appeared about 360 million years ago. Land flora was dominated by seed ferns at this time. Amphibians could be found 340 million years ago. The development of enclosed eggs in early reptiles about 320 million years ago freed animals from watery environments and led to the later evolution of mammals and dinosaurs, as well as flying and swimming reptiles.

The earliest reptiles evolved from amphibians about 305 million years ago. Around 280 million years ago we find the earliest beetles. In this same time frame seed plants and conifers diversified greatly. This, in turn, led the way for dinosaurs to evolve about 225 million years ago, and the first mammals evolved from reptiles about 215 million years ago undergoing a major evolutionary leap from egg-laying to giving live birth. Dinosaurs didn't go completely extinct 65.5 million years ago— they survive today as birds, whose distinctive wings, feathers, and other features are visible in transitional fossils such as Archaeopteryx from about 150 million years ago.

The first flowering plants evolved 130 million years ago. These plants attracted insects to spread pollen, which in turn led to a major burst in animal evolution. The first ants and termites evolved about 80 million years ago. Early mammals did not lay low under the shadows of dinosaurs; they exploited promising niches, evolving traits that led to their adaptive explosion after the extinction of the dinosaurs.

Primates began to appear in the fossil record about 75 million years ago. The evolution of tree-dwelling primates to upright-walking apes led to the evolution of modern humans. Apes began to appear about 28 million years ago; however, the great apes (in the family hominidae) began to appear about 15 million years ago, speciating from the gibbons (lesser apes). The homininae subfamily began to appear about 8 million years ago, their ancestors having speciated from the ancestors of the orangutan about 13 million years ago, and the hominini tribe speciated from the homininae (the ancestors of the gorillas) about 10 million years ago. The *Homo* genus (our ancestors) began to appear about 2.6 million years ago. The earliest evidence of stone tools was found at Gona in Ethiopia in 1994. The artifacts have been securely dated to 2.6 million years and were clearly manufactured, as opposed to shapes formed naturally by erosion or being tumbled in streams.

The species *Homo sapiens* began to appear about 500,000 years ago and the sub-species *Homo sapiens sapiens* (humans) began to appear about 200,000 years ago with the first evidence of their existence found in Africa. There was a catastrophic eruption of Mount Toba on the island of Sumatra 74,000 years ago, dropping the planet into a five-year winter and continuing with a 19,000-year ice age. Many species were wiped out. This event caused a population crash among prehistoric humans, finishing off some populations and paving the way for the spread of modern humanity.

Recent genetic studies suggest that all of today's humans descended from approximately 10,000 North African ancestors who lived some 60,000 years ago. An exodus from Africa over the Arabian Peninsula around 60,000 years ago brought modern humans to Eurasia, with one group rapidly settling coastal areas around the Indian Ocean and one group migrating north to steppes of Central Asia. Migration from the Black Sea area into Europe started some 45,000 years ago, probably along the Danubian corridor. By 20,000 years ago, the whole of Europe was settled. Cro-Magnons (cave dwellers) were early *Homo sapiens sapiens* of the Upper Paleolithic (late stone-age) in Europe. The earliest known remains of Cro-Magnon like humans are radiometrically dated to 35,000 years ago. The Cro-Magnons were among the first known artists as well as hunter-gatherers who exhibited degrees of spiritual awareness, social interaction, and fluid intelligence.

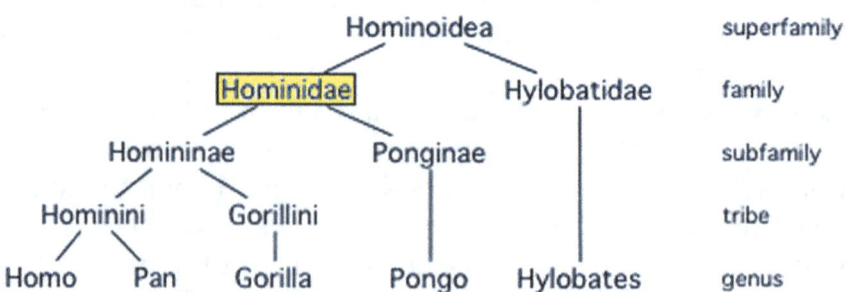

**Family tree showing the extant hominoids:** humans (genus *Homo*), chimpanzees (genus *Pan*), gorillas (genus *Gorilla*), orangutans (genus *Pongo*) and gibbons (four genera of the family Hylobatidae: *Hylobates*, *Hoolock*, *Nomascus*, and *Symphalangus*). All except gibbons are hominids. (Ref.: http://en.wikipedia.org/wiki/Hominidae)

Hopefully the above gives the reader a clearer view of the evolution of life. Thanks to modern science it is now possible to establish somewhat realistic dates for the evolution of the various species. While the dates provided herein may lead you to think that changes happened abruptly, that is not the case. The evolutionary process is a slow and steady process. The rough dates given are just snapshots along the evolutionary timeline. The processes for dating artifacts have improved remarkably in recent years. Even so, different references, especially older ones, don't always agree with the dates given above, but the picture is clear as it was to Charles Darwin that species evolve over time through the process of natural selection adaptive to their environments. Organisms most suited to their environment survive and reproduce, passing on their advantageous traits to offspring. Organisms that cannot compete go extinct.

Through evolution, new species arise through the process of speciation, where new varieties of organisms arise and thrive when they are able to find and exploit an ecological niche, and species become extinct when they are no longer able to survive in changing conditions or against superior competition. A typical species becomes extinct within 10 million years of its first appearance, although some species, referred to as living fossils, survive virtually unchanged for hundreds of millions of years. Most extinctions have occurred naturally, prior to *Homo sapiens* walking on Earth: it is estimated that 99.9% of all species that have ever existed are now extinct.

Mass extinctions are relatively rare events; however, isolated extinctions are quite common. Most species that become extinct are never scientifically documented. Only recently have extinctions been recorded and scientists have become alarmed at the high rates of recent extinctions. A major extinction event is currently in process commencing 30,000 to 40,000 years ago with the expansion of modern humans. Some scientists estimate that up to half of presently existing species may become extinct by 2100. It is difficult to estimate the trajectory that biodiversity might have taken without human impact but scientists at the University of Bristol estimate that biodiversity might increase exponentially without human influence.

Darwin noticed that the seed-crushing bills of little songbirds called finches were adapted to various niches throughout the Galapagos Islands. This proved integral to the formulation of Darwin's theory of evolution by natural selection. And the birds haven't stopped evolving. For example, the medium ground finch (*Geospiza fortis*), in recent years downsized its beak to exploit small seeds more efficiently after a larger finch arrived on its island and began competing for food. The smaller beaks on the smaller birds allowed them to thrive, while the big birds ate all the big seeds and nearly went extinct. Some more recent observations also show evolution at work. Australian lizards called skinks are dropping their limbs to be more like snakes. When studying their embryos stubs can be found where limbs once existed. Some varieties of skinks have turned snaky in just 3.6 million years, relatively fast in evolutionary terms. Another example is a toxic toad introduced in 1936 to wipe out a beetle species wreaking havoc on Australia's sugar cane crop. The toad has itself become a pest, evolving longer legs to help it hop across the country at an ever-increasing rate. The added leg length gives more speed, which permits the longer-legged toads to secure the best habitats at newly conquered terrains. Genome analyses and the understanding of genetic mutation have led scientists to now accept Darwin's theory of evolution as fact.

About 65.5 million years ago a large meteor struck Earth in the Yucatan peninsula. This, coupled with high volcanic activity in India, caused the extinction of over half of the animal species, including the dinosaurs. Birds by this time had evolved from dinosaurs and many birds did survive the extinction event. The extinction of the dinosaurs paved the way for mammals to become the dominant species.

Trying to understand our human origins has always been a fundamental part of who we are. One of the core things we want to know is how we came to be. The human story begins in one of the most geologically fascinating areas on Earth, the Great Rift Valley of Africa. It is an enormous split torn into Earth's crust that runs from the forests in Tanzania to the deserts of Ethiopia. In some places the rift is thousands of feet deep and exposes the last 15 million years of Earth's history. Here, fossil remains of our earliest ancestors can be found. Humankind appears to have first evolved in Africa, as the fossils of early humans (*hominids*) who lived between 5 million and 2 million years ago come entirely from Africa.

Let's now track the evolution of *Hominini* to *Homo* (humans). *Ardipithecus* was a very early pre-hominin ape or ape-hominin transitional species at about 4.4 million years ago. Fossils for other pre-hominin apes and ape transitional species go back to around 7 million years ago. *Ardipithecus* had a small brain about the same size as a bonobo monkey's brain. The four little toes on each foot were adapted for walking on the ground. Yet the big toe was still opposable, much like our thumbs. This sort of big toe helped *Ardipithecus* move through the trees.

*Australopithecus afarensis* lived between 3.9 and 2.9 million years ago, walked bi-pedally, and is most likely the ancestor to both the genus *Australopithecus* and the genus *Homo*. The brain size was slightly larger than *Ardipithecus*. *Australopithecus* means Southern ape, referring to South Africa, where the initial fossils were found.

*Kenyanthropus platyops* is a fossil that was discovered in Lake Turkana, Kenya, in 1999 by Justus Erus. It evolved from the *Australopithecus* in the savannas of Africa around 3.5 million years ago. The fossil found features a broad flat face with a toe bone that suggests it probably walked upright. Teeth are intermediate between typical human and typical ape forms. *Australopithecines* evolved shortly thereafter. The fossil Lucy is *australopithecines*. It is a partial skeleton (3.2 million years old) found by Donald Johanson and colleagues, who, in celebration of their find, played the Beatles song *Lucy in the Sky with Diamonds* over and over—thus the name Lucy.

The genus *Homo* evolved about 2.5 million years ago. *Homo habilis* (handy man) evolved about 2.3 million years ago. *Homo habilis* was short and had disproportionately long arms compared to modern humans; however, it had a less protruding face than the *australopithecines* from which it is thought to have descended. *Homo habilis* had a cranial capacity slightly less than half of the size of modern humans. Despite the ape-like morphology of the bodies, *Homo habilis* remains are often accompanied by primitive stone tools. *Homo rudolfensis* (Rudolf man) evolved about 1.9 million years ago. Fossils found in Kenya indicate that this species had a face and body that were larger than the predecessor *Homo habilis* and it had larger teeth, but it also had human-like features, including a relatively large brain size. Also about 1.9 million years ago, *Homo habilis* was followed by the lankier and more sophisticated *Homo ergastor* (working man); they coexisted for close to a million years. The first stone tools began to appear during this timeframe.

*Homo erectus* (upright man) evolved in Africa about 1.8 million years ago and had a brain size about three-fourths that of modern man. The first human settlement existed in Africa as early as 800,000 years ago. *Homo antecessor* (predecessor man) lived about 1.2 to 0.8 million years ago. *Homo heidlebergensis* (Heidelberg man), at about 600 thousand to 355 thousand years ago, is the common ancestor of Neanderthals and *Homo sapiens* (wise man).

Neanderthal man lived about 350,000 to 30,000 years ago with an average brain size slightly larger than that of modern humans. The hardy Neanderthals lived and hunted successfully in Europe despite the bitter grip of the last Ice Age 100,000 plus years ago. It has been determined that they had the capacity to speak. A "first draft" of the Neanderthal genome has been prepared by scientists with the Max Planck Institute in Germany, and there is evidence there was interbreeding between Neanderthals and modern humans about 80,000 years ago. Modern humans and Neanderthals trace a common ancestry to sometime before 250,000 years ago. People of European descent can have up to 4% Neanderthal genes in their DNA. Modern humans share about 99% of their DNA with Neanderthals and slightly less with chimpanzees, our closest living evolutionary relative. Another interesting tidbit is that recent comparisons of the genomes of chimpanzees, mice, and humans revealed all three have about 30,000 genes and that the human genome shares close to 98% of its genes with chimpanzees and mice. Human ancestors and mice diverged about 75 million years ago. Human ancestors and chimpanzees diverged between 6 and 7 million years ago.

# Comparative Table of Homo Species

Adapted from: http://en.wikipedia.org/wiki/Homo_(genus)

| Species | Million years ago lived | Where | Adult height | Adult mass | Cranial capacity (cm³) | Fossil record |
|---|---|---|---|---|---|---|
| *H. antecessor* | 1.2 – 0.8 | Spain | 1.75 m (5.7 ft) | 90 kg (200 lb) | 1,000 | 2 sites |
| *H. cepranensis* | 0.9 – 0.8 | Italy | | | 1,000 | 1 skull cap |
| *H. erectus* | 1.8 – 0.2 | Africa, Eurasia (Java, China, India, Caucasus) | 1.8 m (5.9 ft) | 60 kg (130 lb) | 850 (early) – 1,100 (late) | Many |
| *H. ergaster* | 1.9 – 1.4 | Eastern and Southern Africa | 1.9 m (6.2 ft) | | 700–850 | Many |
| *H. floresiensis* | 0.10 – 0.012 | Indonesia | 1.0 m (3.3 ft) | 25 kg (55 lb) | 400 | Few |
| *H. gautengensis* | >2 – 0.6 | South Africa | 1.0 m (3.3 ft) | | | 1 individual |
| *H. georgicus* | 1.8 | Georgia | | | 600 | 4 individuals |
| *H. habilis* | 2.3 – 1.4 | Africa | 1.0–1.5 m (3.3–4.9 ft) | 33–55 kg (73–120 lb) | 510–660 | Many |
| *H. heidelbergensis* | 0.6 – 0.35 | Europe, Africa, China | 1.8 m (5.9 ft) | 60 kg (130 lb) | 1,100–1,400 | Many |
| *H. neanderthalensis* | 0.35 – 0.03 | Europe, Western Asia | 1.6 m (5.2 ft) | 55–70 kg (120–150 lb) (heavily built) | 1,200–1,900 | Many |
| *H. rhodesiensis* | 0.3 – 0.12 | Zambia | | | 1,300 | Very few |
| *H. rudolfensis* | 1.9 | Kenya | | | | Very few |
| *H. sapiens idaltu* | 0.16 – 0.15 | Ethiopia | | | 1,450 | 3 craniums |
| *H. sapiens sapiens* (modern humans) | 0.2 – present | Worldwide | 1.4–1.9 m (4.6–6.2 ft) | 50–100 kg (110–220 lb) | 1,000–1,850 | Still living |

Mitochondrial Eve, a hypothetical human being, lived in sub-Saharan East Africa about 200 thousand years ago and is the furthest back female ancestor common to all mitochondrial lineages in humans alive today. Y-chromosomal Adam also lived in Africa and is the furthest back common male ancestor of all modern humans. It took over 100,000 years before our *Homo sapiens* ancestors finally left the African cradle in their successive waves of migrations. Some modern humans migrated to South Asia about 50 thousand years ago and to Australia and Europe about 40 thousand years ago. Some eventually came to North America from Siberia across the Bering Strait by island-hopping through the Aleutians about 30 thousand years ago. The Neanderthal linage died out about 27,000 years ago; however, modern humans and Neanderthals coexisted for thousands of years. The evolutionary path to modern humans has been slow and steady. The fossils found provide snapshots in time of the evolutionary process. Today's humans are a part of an evolutionary family tree that includes at least 16 now-extinct humanlike species. The late Harvard biologist Stephen Jay Gould was probably right to observe that we all come from the same African twig on the bushy tree of human evolution.

The Roman poet Ovid wrote, "Every shape that's born bears in its womb the seeds of change." This phrase is prophetically apt when one considers the constant change of living things as revealed by the fossil record. Earliest life on Earth was microbial and unicellular. Change produced multicellular organisms, and these increased in complexity to form a vast array of invertebrates. For a time, invertebrates were the only members of the animal kingdom. Then fishes appeared, and with the further passage of time, amphibians, reptiles, mammals and birds became established on Earth. Within each of these taxonomic classes, change continued, endlessly increasing the diversity of life. And yet, throughout the millions of transmutations that led to diversity, there has been a common thread, for all living creatures are descendants of forms that lived in the past. No matter how seemingly different, every organism exhibits basic similarities in its solutions to fundamental life processes. The paleontologists, who study the fossils in successively younger sequences of strata, can recognize the constant attributes of all life and also see changes unfold through time.

Life on Earth has been evolving for close to 4 billion years. After our universe became rich in certain basic elements, some of those elements got together to form basic molecules and in successive steps these molecules became more and more complex. Finally, in some extraordinary chemical process, life evolved. During Earth's history, there have been about 10 billion species. As far as we can tell, only one, *Homo sapiens sapiens*, has reached this level of intelligence. The evolution of intelligence requires a highly evolved brain and probably an advanced visual system as well. One thing for certain—life forms will continue to evolve. We are just a snapshot in the continuing timeline of life. Which directions evolution will take in the future we can only speculate. The evolutionary process for life has proceeded from very simple to complex. There is no reason to think this pattern will not continue in the future. Evolutionary development is driven by natural selection to specific environmental conditions and by chance factors such as mutations. Gene mutations can be good or bad. Natural selection works to promote reproductive success above all else. In this manner bad mutations tend to be eliminated or minimized while good mutations lead to more reproductive success adaptive to particular environments. Life forms will likely continue to become more complex over the eons of time. Change is inevitable. Evolution is inevitable.

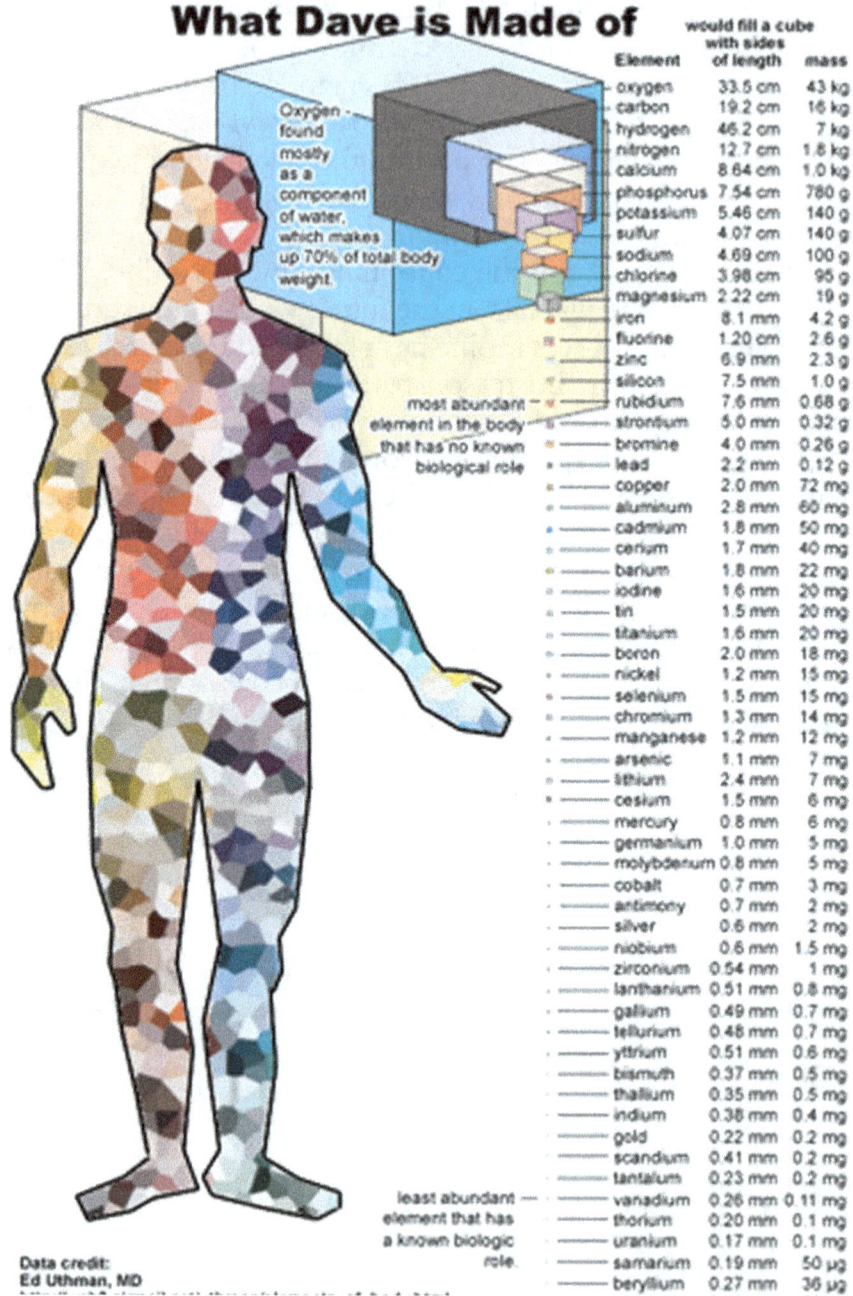

Retrieved from:
http://scienceblogs.com/startswithabang/2011/09/how_stable_
is_the_stuff_were_m.php

Raw data from which the above table was made are from Emsley, John, *The Elements*, 3rd ed., Clarendon Press, Oxford, 1998.

Researchers from the University of Chicago analyzed the genomes of 209 unrelated individuals from three distinct human populations: East Asians, Europeans, and Yorubans from Nigeria. Each population contained roughly 250 positively selected genes, with many of the selected genes differing depending on the group. The study addressed the question of whether humans are still evolving and the answer was an absolute yes. The study also linked genetic changes to major events in the history of our species such as the advent of agriculture, shifts in diet, new habitats, and climatic changes over the past 10,000 years. Many genes were found to be evolving in all three of the human populations studied. The specific functions of many of the genes are not known, but the researchers were able to separate them into broad categories. These categories include:

- Olfaction: the researchers found many genes important for taste and smell,
- Reproduction: involved in things like sperm mobility and egg fertilization,
- Increasing brain size,
- Carbohydrate metabolism: positive selection was observed for genes involved in breaking down mannose (a sweet secretion found in some trees and shrubs) in Yorubans, sucrose in East Asians, and lactose for Europeans,
- Disease resistance and pathogen protection, and
- Metabolism of foreign components, such as exotic plant proteins or animal toxins.

The researchers also found positive selection in four pigment genes important for lighter skin in Europeans that were not previously known. Scientists believe humans evolved lighter skin in Europe as an adaptation to less sunlight. In East Asians, they found strong evidence of positive selection in genes involved in the production of alcohol dehydrogenase (ADH), a protein necessary for breaking down alcohol. Many East Asians can't metabolize alcohol because they carry a mutation that prevents them from making ADH.

It is clear that evolution is an intrinsic and proper characteristic of our universe. Neither our universe as a whole nor any of its ingredients can be understood except in terms of evolution. Evolution is a daily happening. We, for instance, are constantly exchanging atoms with the total reservoir of atoms in our universe. Each year 98% of the atoms in our bodies are renewed. Each time we breathe we take in billions and billions of atoms recycled by breathing organisms during the past few weeks. Nothing in our genes was present a year ago. It is all new, regenerated from the available energy and matter in our universe. A person's skin is renewed each month and the liver each six weeks. Human beings are among the most recycled beings in our universe. With more people crowding into ever more ecological niches over the past 10,000 years, humans appear to be evolving more rapidly than in the distant past. Also, as people have adapted to different regions, cultures, and diets, they have become increasingly different from people elsewhere. For example, Europeans have evolved a tolerance for dairy products into adulthood, whereas people in China and most of Africa have not.

An *Essay on the Principle of Population*, which was written by the Reverend Thomas Malthus, an Anglican clergyman, and first published in 1798, created overpopulation alarmism. The gist of his case was that humans, like other forms of life, tended to reproduce in numbers greater than could be easily supported by available resources. This mismatch between population and resources generated poverty, crime, and greed. True, periods of relief occasionally would occur after plagues had sharply reduced population or technological breakthroughs had abruptly increased available resources (especially food); but the power of population was so great that soon there again would be too many people. Population might eventually stabilize, but it would do so at a level above that of "easy support." Relief from social problems, then, would be rare and temporary.

Malthus' claim that population tended to stabilize at a level greater than what resources could easily support meant there would be not only social problems, but also nearly constant pressure for culture change. As he wrote toward the end of his essay, the press of population "is constantly acting upon man as a powerful stimulus, urging him to the further cultivation of the earth, and to enable it consequently to support a more extended population." Malthus did see some hope. He stated: "The exertions that men find it necessary to make, in order to support themselves or families, frequently awaken faculties that might otherwise have lain forever dormant, and it has been commonly remarked that new and extraordinary situations generally create minds adequate to grapple with the difficulties in which they are involved." Let's hope Malthus was right about mankind's ingenuity.

In 1968 Paul Ehrlich, a Stanford University population biologist, predicted that because of the ever-growing population "hundreds of millions of people are going to starve to death," and it was too late to do anything about it. This prediction has been delayed somewhat with the green revolution—a combination of high-yield seeds, irrigation, pesticides, and fertilizers that has enabled grain production to double (a tribute to mankind's ingenuity). Today many people are undernourished, but mass starvation is rare.

After World War II, developing countries got a sudden transfusion of preventive care with the help of institutions like the World Health Organization and UNICEF. Penicillin, the smallpox vaccine, and DDT (which, though later controversial, saved millions from dying of malaria)—all came about the same time. Much of the recent population explosion is due to longer life expectancy. Today, an average of 2.1 births per woman would maintain a steady population in developed countries. Still, many people are justifiably worried that Malthus and Ehrlich will finally be proven right on a global scale. Food and fresh water shortages could cause a collapse of global civilization. Human beings are living off natural capital, with soil eroding and groundwater depleting faster than they can be replenished. At some point this could well put the whole world on a wartime footing.

The growing human population is currently on a crash course with an eroding and depleting environment. One of the great frontiers is going to be trying to keep humans alive in a much more toxic world. Hopefully human ingenuity can continue to come to the rescue. In 1960, the world population reached three billion. By 2011, it more than doubled to seven billion. By 2045, it is expected to reach nine billion. The world population will have tripled during the average human lifespan.

# Growth of Human Population

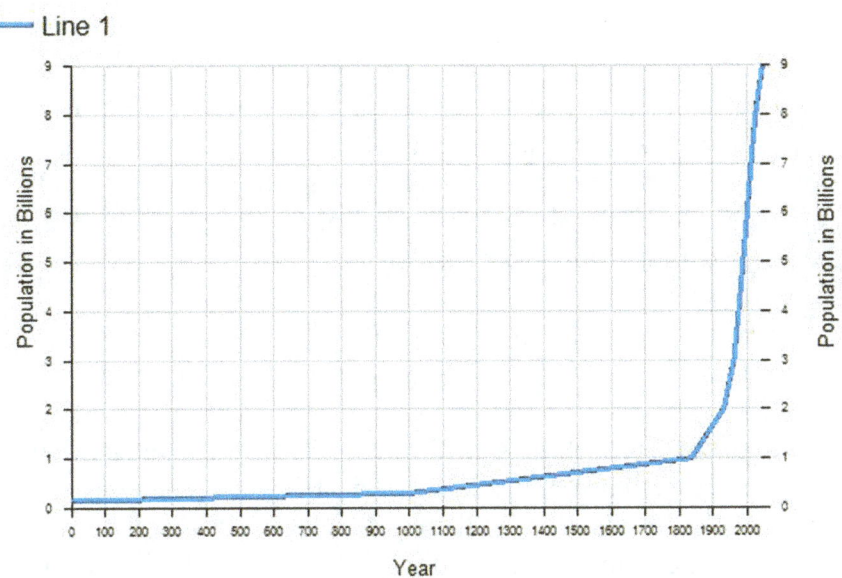

## Year

| Year | |
|---|---|
| 8000 BC | Human population estimated at 5 million. |
| 1 AD | Human population estimated at 150 million. |
| 1000 AD | Human population estimated at 300 million. |
| 1835 AD | Human population reaches 1 billion. |
| 1930 AD | Human population reaches 2 billion. |
| 1960 AD | Human population reaches 3 billion. |
| 1974 AD | Human population reaches 4 billion. |
| 1987 AD | Human population reaches 5 billion. |
| 1999 AD | Human population reaches 6 billion. |
| 2011 AD | Human population reaches 7 billion. |
| 2024 AD | Human population projected to reach 8 billion. |
| 2045 AD | Human population projected to reach 9 billion. |

(Data from January 2011 *National Geographic Magazine* article titled "Population 7 Billion.")

Mega destructive events can affect evolution of life as it adapts to changed environments. So what are the natural threats to human beings? Sixty-five million years ago a large asteroid 60 miles across struck the Yucatan peninsula in Mexico. This, combined with gases from exploding volcanoes, caused destruction of much foliage and extinction of non-avian dinosaurs. Such a threat continues to exist. Other natural threats include mega earthquakes, mega tsunamis, mega volcanoes, and mega storms sometimes referred to as ARk storms. (In 1861-62 an "Atmospheric River" brought California 45 straight days of rain and caused flooding of biblical proportions, evocative of Noah and his ark).

Thirteen centuries ago Maya priests predicted the end of an era on December 21, 2012 (interpreted by some as an apocalypse). This day marks the end of a Maya 5200 year era and the end of the thirteenth 144,000 day cycle in the Maya calendar. There was an abrupt climatic event 5,200 years ago which had a large impact on lives and cultures. This event coincided with the end of another Maya era, "the fourth Sun," and the beginning of a new era, "the fifth Sun." While we really don't know what the Maya priests had in mind, we do know that a natural phenomena will occur. On December 21, 2012 at 11:12 GMT, the Milky Way galaxy center, the sun, and Earth will be in alignment. This occurs once every 26,000 years. The beginning of the Maya "first Sun" coincided with the previous alignment 26,000 years ago. According to the Maya, the center of the galaxy is the cosmic womb, the place of dead, transformation, regeneration, and re-birth.

Approximately every eleven years the sun's magnetic poles flip. This happened in 1859, knocking out telegraph service. Other flips have occurred which were hardly noticeable, the last being in February 2001. The next flip is due in 2012. "This always happens around the time of solar maximum," says David Hathaway, a solar physicist at the Marshall Space Flight Center. "The magnetic poles exchange places at the peak of the sunspot cycle. In fact, it's a good indication that Solar Max is really here." If such an occurrence as the 1859 solar "super storm" were to happen in 2012, our power grid could be severely damaged and satellite circuitry fried. To repair the damage could take years with profound effects on our lives; however, this would not be an apocalypse. Astronomers and NASA scientists have been quick to stress that there is nothing to be concerned about; December 21, 2012 will be just another ordinary winter solstice. While predictions for an apocalypse make for some intriguing television viewing, it is very unlikely that the Maya priests were better than today's astronomers and NASA scientists at predicting such outcomes

Earth's magnetic field also flips, but with less regularity than the sun's. Reversals on Earth occur roughly every 500,000 years. The last reversal happened 740,000 years ago. Some researchers think our planet is overdue for another one, but nobody knows exactly when the next reversal might occur. We do know that as Earth approaches a reversal, its magnetic field decreases, and it has by 5% since 1832, so a reversal is nearing. The effect of these reversals can vary greatly. We are currently unable to predict their outcomes. However, considering that the reversal for Earth is gradual, there likely will not be any major short-term consequences.

In this era of greatly escalating science and technology, along with a growing population, man-made threats are just as worrisome as natural threats. Many biologists believe that at the current rate of human destruction of the biosphere, one-half of all current species of life will be extinct in 100 years. Emerging biotechnologies, such as genomics and nanotechnology, will make it possible for those with bad intentions to alter bacteria and viruses to increase their lethality, and the use of weapons of mass destruction could eliminate large populations.

To end this chapter on a more positive note, consider that a good part of our destiny is ours to control. Through evolving science and technology we may well be able to deflect dangers from space and to control the weather here on this Earth. We are becoming better at predicting earthquakes and volcanic activity so that hopefully in the future we will be able to sidestep their destructive forces. While science and technology have led to many positive innovations toward healthier more comfortable lives, future years will bring even more innovations at an ever increasing rate.

# Timeline of Important Events in the Evolution of Life

| Years ago | Event |
|---|---|
| 13.7 billion +/- 1% | "Big Bang" origination of our universe and time in our universe. |
| 13.2 billion +/- .8% | Our Milky Way galaxy formed |
| 4.9-4.8 billion | Our solar system formed. |
| 4.8-4.7 billion | Our sun became an active star. |
| 4.567 billion +/- .2% | Formation of solid Earth by accretion. |
| 4.3 billion | Earth melts due to radioactive and gravitational heating yielding its differential interior structure and outgassing of molecules such as water, methane, ammonia, hydrogen, nitrogen, and carbon dioxide. |
| 4.3 billion | Atmospheric water is photodissociated by ultraviolet light yielding oxygen atoms that are incorporated into an ozone layer and hydrogen atoms that escape into space. |
| 3.8 billion | Earth's crust solidifies forming oldest rocks. Also, atmospheric water condenses into oceans. Earth temps now below 100° C. |
| 3.5 billion | Sediments in NW Australia record a shallow marine environment, i.e., fossils of filamentous prokaryotes Cyanabacterium. (Therefore, unicellular bacterial life goes back 3.5 billion years.) |
| 3.5-2.8 billion | Beginning of photosynthesis by blue-green algae releasing oxygen molecules into atmosphere strengthening the ozone layer. |
| 2.2-1.9 billion | Eukaryotic cell organizations originate. |
| 1.2 billion | Simple multicellular algae evolve. |

| | |
|---|---|
| 1.0 billion | Super continent Rodinia forms, then brakes apart 250 million years later. |
| 600 million | Multicellular organisms such as sponges evolve. |
| **543 million** | **Start of Cambrian period.** |
| 540 million | Trilobites (marine arthropods) evolve. |
| **510 million** | **Transition from Cambrian period to Ordovician period.** First of seven major extinction events occurs (extinction of 75% to 90% of life). |
| 500 million | Vertebrates (fish) evolve. |
| 475 million | First primitive land plants evolve from green algae at lake edges. |
| 450 million | Arthropods evolve (millipedes & centipedes, then spiders & scorpions; were first land animals). |
| 445 million | Second of seven major extinction events occurs (50% of sea species became extinct; probably caused by gamma ray burst from the sun). |
| **439 million** | **Transition from Ordovician period to Silurian period.** |
| 439 million | Vascular dryland plants evolve. |
| 435-353 million | Jawed fish evolve from jawless fish. |
| **409 million** | **Transition from Silurian period to Devonian period.** |
| 375 million | Primitive sharks evolve. |
| 360 million | Super continent Pangaea forms and lasts 120 million years. |
| **354 million** | **Transition from Devonian period to Carboniferous period.** Third of seven major extinctions events occurs. |
| 350 million | Primitive insects evolve. |
| 350 million | Primitive ferns evolve (first plants with roots). |
| 350-300 million | Amphibians evolve. |
| 350-260 million | Reptiles evolve from amphibians. |

| | |
|---|---|
| **300 million** | **Transition from Carboniferous period to Permian period.** |
| 300 million | Winged insects evolve. |
| 280 million | Beetles and weevils evolve. |
| 270-220 million | Therapsids evolve (some of which are ancestors to pre-mammals). |
| **251 million** | **Transition from Permian period to Triassic period.** Fourth major extinction event occurs wiping out about 90% of animal species. |
| 240-100 million | Dinosaurs, crocodilians, pterosaurs, and pre-mammals evolve. |
| 230 million | Birds, roaches, and termites evolve. |
| 225 million | Modern ferns evolve. |
| **206 million** | **Transition from Triassic period to Jurassic period.** Fifth major extinction event occurs. Dinosaurs survive. |
| 145 million | Archaeopteryx (primitive birds of the Jurassic period) evolve. |
| **144 million** | **Transition from Jurassic period to Cretaceous period.** |
| 140 million | Flowering plants evolve. |
| 136 million | Primitive kangaroos evolve. |
| 100 million | Primitive cranes evolve. |
| 90 million | Modern sharks evolve. |
| 88 million | Breakup of Indo-Malagasy land mass. |
| **66 million** | **Transition from Cretaceous period to Tertiary period.** Large asteroid 60 miles across strikes Yucatan peninsula in Mexico. This combined with gases from exploding volcanoes caused destruction of much foliage and extinction of non-avian dinosaurs (sixth major extinction event). |
| 65 million | Early primates evolve. With dinosaurs gone mammals begin their reign. |
| 60 million | Rats, mice, squirrels, herons, and storks evolve. |

| | |
|---|---|
| 55 million | Rabbits and hares evolve. Australia separates from Antarctica. |
| 50 million | Primitive monkeys evolve. |
| 35 million | Grasses evolve. |
| 28 million | Koalas evolve. |
| 22 million | Indian plate collides with Asian plate causing the Himalayan range to rise for past 22 million years. |
| 20 million | African plate collides with Asian plate |
| 20 million | Parrots and pigeons evolve. |
| 20-12 million | Chimpanzees (ape family) evolve. |
| 15 million | Apes (speciated from chimpanzees) migrate from Africa to Eurasia becoming gibbons and orangutans. |
| 14-12 million | *Ramapithecus* evolves. *Ramapithecus* is one of our non-hominid primate ancestors from between 12 and 14 million years ago. Our human ancestors speciated from ancestors of the gibbon. |
| 13-12 million | Hominids evolve. (Chimpanzees and hominids share 98% DNA.) |
| 7 million | Some primates began their move from trees to grasslands. |
| 4 million | Development of hominid bipedalism. |
| 4-1 million | *Australopithecus* (a bipedal hominid) inhabits Earth. |
| 3.5 million | *Australopithecus* "Lucy" walked Earth. |
| 2 million | Widespread use of stone tools. |
| 2 million-10,000 | Most recent ice age. |
| **1.6 million** | **Transition from Tertiary period to Quarternary period.** |
| 1.5 million | *Homo ergaster* evolves. Common ancestor to *Homo erectus* and *Homo heidelbergensis*. |
| 1.9 million | *Homo erectus* evolves. |
| 800,000 | *Homo heidelbergensis* exist (common genetic ancestor of *Homo* |

|  |  |
|---|---|
|  | *neanderthalensis* (Neanderthals) and (humans)). |
| 740,000 | Earth's last (most recent) geomagnetic reversal. |
| 500,000 | *Homo erectus* uses charcoal to control fire in China. *Homo sapiens* evolve. |
| 200,000 | *Homo neanderthalensis* evolve from *Homo heidelbergensis*. *Homo sapiens* evolve with a voice box for vocal communication, allowing them to become greatly more intelligent. |
| 160,000 | Earliest known *Homo sapiens* existed in what is now Ethiopia. |
| 95,000 | *Homo floresiensis* evolve (hobbit-like species of humans that grew no larger than a three-year-old modern child. Named for island of Flores, a southern Indonesian island east of Bali. |
| 74,000 | Catastrophic eruption of Mount Toba on the island of Sumatra dropped the planet into a five-year winter, and continued with a 19,000-year ice age, having a profound effect on life. |
| 28,000 | Neanderthals become extinct. |
| 27,000 | *Homo erectus* becomes extinct. |
| 15,000 | Asians cross over ice sheets to northern North America, becoming the ancestors of the American Indians. |
| 11,000 | *Homo floresiensis* becomes extinct. |
| 10,000 | *Homo sapiens* learn to use fire to cast copper and harden pottery. |
| 6,000 years ago | Writing (cuneiform) is developed in Sumer in Mesopotamia. |
|  | Seventh major extinction event is currently in progress, commencing 30,000 to 40,000 years ago with the expansion of modern humans. The |

observed rate of extinction has risen dramatically over the past 50 years. Many biologists believe that at the current rate of human destruction of the biosphere, one-half of all current species of life will be extinct in 100 years.

# Timeline of Important Events in the Evolution of Life Scaled Down to a Year

We are accustomed to dealing with increments of time measured in minutes, hours, days, weeks, and years. Our history books often examine events over spans of centuries. Geologists routinely deal with time periods in the millions of years and even billions of years. Geologic time is vast. Over millions of years, mountains rise and rivers excavate deep canyons. Earth features, which seem to be everlasting and unchanging to us, are indeed slowly changing. The Earth is continually changing. Our universe is continually changing. The environment and life are evolving.

Astrophysicists have determined our universe to be 13.72 billion years old to within 1%. How long is 13.72 billion years? If you were to begin counting at the rate of one number per second and continued 24 hours a day, 7 days a week, it would take 435 years (about 5 lifetimes) to count to 13.72 billion. Now scale 13.72 billion years down to 1 year. Each second of that scaled down year would then represent 435 actual years. If we look at our universe's history this way, then all of modern science happened in the last second. A timeline of important events would look as follows:

| | |
|---|---|
| January 1 | "Big Bang" originates our universe. |
| January 13 | Our Milky Way galaxy forms. |
| August 22 | Our solar system forms. |
| August 28 | Our sun becomes an active star. |
| August 30 | Solid Earth forms by planetesimal accretion. |
| September 8 | Earth melts due to radioactive and gravitational heat. |
| September 21 | Earth's crust solidifies, forming oldest rocks. |
| September 27 | Unicellular bacterial marine life forms. |
| October 23 | Eukaryotic cell organizations form. |
| November 29 | Simple multicellular algae evolve. |
| December 4 | Super continent Rodinia forms. |

| December 11 | Super continent Rodinia breaks apart. |
| December 16 | Multicellular marine organisms such as sponges evolve. |
| December 17 | Trilobites (marine arthropods) evolve. |
| December 18 | Vertebrates evolve (jawless fish). |
| December 18 | First primitive non-root land plants evolve from algae at lake edges. |
| December 20 | Vascular dry-land plants evolve. |
| December 20 | Jawed fish evolve from jawless fish. |
| December 21 | Primitive sharks evolve. |
| December 22 | Super continent Pangea forms. |
| December 22 | Primitive non-winged insects evolve. |
| December 22 | Primitive ferns evolve (first plants with roots). |
| December 23 | Amphibians evolve. |
| December 23 | Reptiles evolve. |
| December 24 | Winged insects evolve, followed by beetles and weevils. |
| December 25 | Therapsids evolve (some are ancestors to pre-mammals). |
| December 25 | Dinosaurs, crocodilians, pterosaurs, and pre-mammals evolve. |
| December 25 | Birds, roaches, and termites evolve. |
| December 25 | Modern ferns evolve. |
| December 26 | Pangea breaks apart. |
| December 27 | Flowering plants evolve. |
| December 27 | Modern sharks evolve. |
| December 29 | Dinosaurs become extinct and early primates evolve. |
| December 29 | Rats, mice, squirrels, herons, and storks evolve. |
| December 30 | Rabbits, hares, and primitive monkeys evolve. |
| December 30 12 pm | Grasses evolve. |
| December 31 1 am | Koalas evolve. |
| December 31 11 am | Parrots and pigeons evolve. |
| December 31 12 am | Chimpanzees (ape family) evolve. |

| | |
|---|---|
| December 31 2 pm | Gibbons and orangutans evolve from apes. |
| December 31 7 pm | Hominids evolve (Chimpanzees and hominids share 98% DNA). |
| December 31 10 pm | *Australopithecus* ("Lucy") walked Earth. |
| Dec. 31 10:44 pm | *Homo ergaster* evolves (ancestor to *Homo erectus*). |
| Dec. 31 10:45 pm | *Homo erectus* begins to evolve. |
| Dec. 31 11:45 pm | *Homo erectus* uses charcoal to control fire in China. |
| Dec. 31 11:52 pm | *Homo neanderthalensis* evolves. |
| Dec. 31 11:58 pm | *Homo sapiens* (modern humans) evolved in what is now Ethiopia. |
| Dec. 31 11:59:30 pm | Age of Agriculture begins. |
| Dec. 31 11:59:47 pm | Building of the Pyramids. |
| Dec. 31 11:59:58 pm | Jesus is born. |
| Dec. 31 11:59:59 pm | Galileo is born. |
| Dec. 31 12 midnight | Today. |

**World Cultures**

Retrieved from:
http://blogs.cornell.edu/comm3400tt329/files/2010/11/world.jpg

# CHAPTER 3

## Evolution: Cultures and Ethnicity

Culture is a group-specific behavior that is acquired, at least in part, from social influences. It is something that is ever-changing. It is that complex whole that can be seen through the observation and study of language, religion, morals, laws, customs, social and economic organization, art, music, literature, cuisine, stories, myths, ritual practices and beliefs, and many other adaptive traits, characteristics, capabilities, and habits acquired by man as a member of society. Cultures are influenced by the ecological and geographic matrix in which specific groups live. A culture springs from a spirit of place, special times of celebration, daily routines of work and play, ongoing imperatives of relationships, birth, and death.

While there is a wide diversity of cultures, all cultures face the same adaptive imperatives. We give birth; raise, educate, and protect our children and console our elders as they move into their final years. Virtually all cultures endorse most tenets of the Ten Commandments, not because the Judaic world was uniquely inspired, but because they are basic rules that allow a social species to thrive. All cultures create traditions that bring consistency to coupling and procreation. Every culture honors its dead. Given the common challenges, the range and diversity of cultural adaptations is astonishing. One must appreciate the realization that there are many ways of being morally inspired and inherently right. Culture allows us to make sense out of sensations, to find order and meaning in a world that is a hodge-podge of ecological and geographic entities.

The diversity of cultures is a far reaching testament to the variety, and the universality, of the human story. As we drift towards a more homogeneous world, it would be a shame if all human potential were reduced to a single modality, a blandly amorphous generic culture, a monochromatic world of monotony. Throughout history, cultures have come and gone, absorbed by other more powerful societies or eliminated altogether by violence and conquest, famines, or natural disasters. No culture is static. Cultures survive because of their ability to cope with change. Cultures disappear only when they are overwhelmed by external forces, when drastic conditions imposed on them render them incapable of adapting to new possibilities. The grand panorama of cultures of the world is continually changing.

Closely relating to cultures are ethnic groups. An ethnic group is a group of people whose members identify with each other, through a common heritage, often consisting of a common language, a common culture, often including a shared religion, and an ideology that stresses common ancestry. Ethnicity is a fundamental factor in human life: it is a phenomenon inherent in human experience. Many social scientists regard ethnicity as a product of specific kinds of inter-group interactions, rather than an essential quality inherent to human groups. In typical usage, ethnicity denotes a group of people who strongly identify themselves (or are identified by others) as belonging together based on specific common traits they share. The traits are largely involuntary, such as skin color, clan or tribe membership, perceived or actual common ancestry, shared history, or language. Other traits that might delineate an ethnic group include culture, religion or sect, age, caste or social status, speech dialect, place or means of habitation, way of life, and so on.

Throughout history, people have formed communities in order to survive, to thrive, to have social support, and to realize their full potential. Many such communities are viewed and defined as ethnic groups. How many ethnic groups are there in the world? A complete list would be in the thousands, and perhaps tens of thousands. Ethnicity in itself is neither good nor bad. It can be a source of comfort, pride, and belonging.

Cultural evolution as a theory in anthropology was developed in the nineteenth century as an outgrowth of Darwinian evolution. It is the process by which structural reorganization is affected through time, eventually producing a form or structure which is qualitatively different from the ancestral form. It presumes that, over time, cultural change such as the rise of social inequalities or emergence of agriculture occurs as a result of humans adapting to some non-cultural stimulus, such as climate change or population growth. However, unlike Darwinian evolution, cultural evolution is considered directional, which is, as human populations transform themselves, their culture becomes progressively more complex. People at first lived in undifferentiated hordes; then developed social hierarchies with priests, kings, scholars, workers, and so forth; and later accumulated knowledge that was differentiated into the various sciences. In short, human societies evolved, by means of an increasing division of labor, into complex civilizations.

The theory of cultural evolution is an underpinning for other, more complex explanations for cultural change. Social changes are not only driven by biology or a strict adaptation to change but by a complex web of social, environmental, and biological factors. Cultural change can come about due to the environment, due to inventions (and other internal influences), and through contact with others. Cultural evolution is "multilinear"—it is a process consisting of a number of forward paths of different styles and lengths. While specific evolutionary changes are not experienced by all cultures universally, human societies do generally evolve or progress. The primary mechanism for such progress involves technological breakthroughs that make societies more adaptable to and dominant over the environment. Technology here is to be looked at in a broad sense and includes such developments as improvements in tool forms or materials (as with the transition through the Stone, Bronze, and Iron Ages and later the Industrial Revolution), transportation (as from pedestrian to equestrian to motorized forms), and food production (as from hunting and gathering to agriculture). For example, the end of the ice age witnessed the invention of agriculture, which in turn brought about many cultural innovations (such as new rituals and customs that were agriculture-centered) that further changed how people related to nature and, ultimately, each other.

Sub-Saharan Africa is the birthplace of humankind, the cradle of humanity. It is where our hominid, or humanlike, ancestors lived more than four million years ago. Human beings (*Homo sapiens sapiens*) began walking Earth there about 200,000 years ago. Africa is extraordinarily diverse in its geography and cultures, this immense continent measures about 5,000 miles north to south and 4,600 miles east to west. Over the millennia it has given rise to a rich mix of people now inhabiting deserts, rain forests, mountains, and valleys. Within Africa, one finds a wide range of social and political entities. Many diverse cultures have their roots in Africa.

Earth goes through a 26,000 year cycle wobbling on its axis. This "precession" has caused many migrations over many millennia due to climatic changes. About 50,000 years ago, glaciers trapped water in the polar ice caps dropping global sea levels by as much as 300 feet and exposing an overland passageway known as Sundaland. It is a biogeographical region of Southeastern Asia which encompasses the areas of the Asian continental shelf that were exposed during the last ice age. It included the Malay Peninsula on the Asian mainland, as well as the large islands of Borneo, Java, and Sumatra and their surrounding islands. Migrations ensued from Africa, through Southeast Asia, through Sundaland, and across stretches of open sea to both Australia and the highlands of Papua New Guinea which were at that time connected.

Around 45,000 years ago, North Africa and the Middle East were entering a dry spell, and the lush corridor that had made them hospitable for life was becoming a desert. Dependent on game and water, the few humans who had made it to the Middle East were being evicted by climate change. Fortunately for them, the mountains to their east provided a much needed refuge. From there humans began their migration into central Asia where they settled about 40,000 years ago and where they thrived.

Around 35,000 years ago, migration originating in and around the fertile Altai Mountains of southern Siberia brought people to the inhospitable reaches of the Arctic. Shorter, stockier frames better equipped for the frigid weather became the norm and are retained in today's Arctic populations. To better survive the harsh environment the people of the Arctic began using skins of their prey for clothing and shelter.

Around 30,000 years ago the Eurasian steppe lands extended from present day Germany, and possibly France, to Korea and China. The climate fostered a land rich in resources and opened a window into Europe for the first wave of modern humans to colonize the region. These inventive early humans in Europe are named the Cro-Magnon after the cave where the first specimens were found in southwest France. Their emergence heralded an end to the era of the Neanderthals, a hominid species that inhabited Europe and parts of western Asia from about 250,000 to 25,000 years ago. It is thought that the better communication skills, weapons, and resourcefulness of the Cro-Magnon probably allowed them to out-compete Neanderthals for scarce resources. Considering the importance of Central Asia as a staging ground for human dispersal, one could say that if Africa was the cradle of humanity, then central Asia was its nursery.

In Africa, climate is controlled by the intertropical convergence zone, a belt of low pressure created by the upwelling of hot moist air above and below the equator. This system produces both equatorial rainfall and incredibly arid conditions to its north and south, resulting in today's Sahara and Kalahari deserts. However, because of Earth's precession cycle, the convergence zone migrates by about 20° in latitude causing dramatic changes in climate patterns. Seven thousand years ago we know these deserts were verdant with tall grasses and acacia woodlands, with a wide variety of grazing herbivores. The analysis of DNA from populations throughout North Africa and the Middle East confirms that when climate shifted, our ancestors headed for greener pastures. Similar migrations have also occurred due to glacial ice advancing and receding. During the glacial maximum the sea levels dropped by as much as 300 feet, providing a Bering land bridge. This enabled hardy individuals to begin migrating from

Northeast Asia to North America beginning about 20,000 years ago, with some continuing down into South America over the next 10,000 years. As peoples settled the various niches of the world, they took on their own cultures and ethnicity.

Today, Asia is home to more ethnic groups than any other major region. These groups have evolved over a very long time, some developing in isolation while others have complex histories of interaction and sharing either through peaceful migration or military conquest. China, India, and Indonesia are home to 40% of Earth's people. Indonesia alone counts more than 700 languages, India over 400, and China more than 200; however, Korea is home to only one language. In South Asia, the nations of India, Pakistan, Bangladesh, Bhutan, Nepal, and Sri Lanka share an ethnic background and all have similar cultures. This is largely due to the fact that, before the 1947 partition, India included both Pakistan and Bangladesh in its borders. The reason they were separated was due to differing religious beliefs. In Africa, the populace also speaks hundreds of languages and, if dialects spoken by various ethnic groups are also included, the number is much higher. All these languages and dialects are not of the same importance though, as some have only a few hundred speakers while others have millions. Among the most prominent languages in Africa are Arabic, Swahili and Hausa. Very few countries of Africa use any single language and this is the reason why several African official languages often coexist.

Europe, over the course of many millennia, has witnessed astonishing cultural development. While half the size of North America, streams of influential ideas, technologies, political and legal structures, works of art, literature, music, and other products of human endeavor have poured forth into the rest of the world. Europe and its remarkably diverse peoples have engendered and nurtured many of the ideals that inform and inspire modern society and culture.

While human beings have been walking Earth for about 200,000 years ago, it has been only about 10,000 years ago that our distant ancestors began establishing and living within larger and more complex communities. A move to agriculture, at the end of the last ice age, rapidly changed the course of human culture. It allowed for higher population densities, stratified societal complexes, and warfare. We live in an elaborate system composed of governing bodies, detailed laws, dense urban centers, elaborate trade networks, visual and written cultures, class structures, militaries, and more. Our world is indebted to a host of early civilizations that paved the way for our current ways of life, including the Sumerians, the ancient Egyptians, the Chinese, and the Maya. Without the critical strides they made in areas of government, law, trade, social hierarchies, culture, and more, human civilization as we know it today would not even exist. State formation didn't happen in one area and then spread outward. Instead, the emergence of states and regional civilizations occurred throughout the ancient world, from the fertile valleys of the Near East and the savannahs of Africa to the Pacific coast of South America and the plains of China.

The ancient Sumerian civilization took form between 4500 and 4000 BC in southern Mesopotamia (modern Iraq). Sumer was the first civilization to practice intensive, year-round agriculture showing the use of core agricultural techniques, including large-scale intensive cultivation of land, organized irrigation, and the use of a specialized labor force. The surplus of storable food created by this economy allowed the population to settle in one place, instead of migrating after crops and grazing land. It also allowed for a much greater population density, and, in turn, required an extensive labor force and division of labor. Sumer was also the site of early development of writing. There is also much evidence that the Sumerians loved music. It seemed to be an important part of religious and civic life in Sumer. The Sumerians developed a complex system of metrology around 4000 BC, resulting in the creation of arithmetic, geometry, and algebra.

Ancient Egyptian civilization is considered as one of the oldest in the history of mankind. The pyramids of Ancient Egypt are still considered as wonders of the world in the twenty-first century. The treasures discovered from the pyramids and other monuments shed much light on Ancient Egyptian culture. The greatness of this civilization is that it had three thousand years of continuous history. The Ancient Egyptian civilization began around 3150 BC, as the result of the political unification of the major Nile Valley civilizations. Pharaohs were the rulers. After passing through many golden ages and powerful kingdoms of Pharaohs, the era of Ancient Egyptian civilization ended with the death of legendary queen Cleopatra.

Life in ancient Egypt depended largely on the Nile River. The farmers of that age are known for their use of irrigation systems. Ancient Egyptian language was at one point the longest surviving and used language. It was used from 3000 BC to the eleventh century. Their writing system was made up of pictures (hieroglyphs). The laws were made and maintained by the Pharaohs and were based on a common-sense view of right and wrong. The ancient Egyptian polytheistic religion was followed for more than ten thousand years until the establishment of Christianity and Islam. The beliefs and rituals developed, changed, and merged with time depending on the ruling families. Ancient Egyptians worshiped a vast array of gods with supposedly many different powers. Pharaohs were considered as the connections between material and spiritual realms. A variety of games, music and other leisure activities such as hunting and boating were enjoyed by ancient Egyptians.

Ancient Greece is the civilization belonging to the period of Greek history lasting from the Archaic period of the eighth to sixth centuries BC to the end of antiquity and beginning of the Early Middle Ages with the rise of the Byzantine era. At the center of this time period is Classical Greece, which flourished during the fifth to fourth centuries BC, at first under Athenian leadership successfully repelling the military threat of Persian invasion. The Athenian Golden Age ends with the defeat of Athens at the hands of Sparta in the Peloponnesian War in 404 BC. Following the conquests of Alexander the Great, Hellenistic civilization flourished from Central Asia to the western end of the Mediterranean Sea.

Classical Greek culture had a powerful influence on the Roman Empire, which carried a version of it to many parts of the Mediterranean region and Europe, for which reason Classical Greece is generally considered to be the seminal culture that provided the foundation of Western civilization. The civilization of ancient Greece has been immensely influential on, politics, educational systems, philosophy, science, and the arts. Via the Roman Empire, Greek culture came to be foundational to Western culture in general.

The ancient Roman Empire was a thriving civilization that grew on the Italian Peninsula as early as the eighth century BC. Located along the Mediterranean Sea and centered on the city of Rome, it became one of the largest empires in the ancient world. In its centuries of existence, Roman civilization shifted from a monarchy to an aristocratic republic to an increasingly autocratic empire. It came to dominate Southern Europe, Western Europe, the Balkans, Asia Minor, North Africa, and parts of Eastern Europe through conquest and assimilation. Rome was preponderant throughout the Mediterranean region and was the sole superpower of Antiquity. Even today its influence survives.

A society highly developed in military and politics, Rome professionalized the military and created a system of government that became the inspiration for most of today's republics. By the end of the republic, Rome had conquered more than the half of the known world at that time, its domain extending from the Atlantic to Judaea and from the mouth of the Rhine to North Africa.

Rome entered into its golden times at the hands of Augustus Caesar. Ancient Rome contributed greatly to government, law, war, art, literature, architecture, technology, religion, and language in the Western world. Its history continues to have a major influence on the world today.

A culture, like an individual, is a more or less consistent pattern of thought and action. Within each culture there comes into being characteristic purposes not necessarily shared by other societies. In obedience to their purposes, each culture further and further consolidates its experience, and in proportion to the urgency of these drives, the heterogeneous items of behavior take more and more congruous shape. Taken up by a well-integrated culture, the most ill-assorted acts become characteristic of the society's particular goals, often by the most unlikely metamorphoses. Cultures are internally affected by both forces encouraging change and forces resisting change. These forces are related to both social structures and natural events, and are involved in the perpetuation of cultural ideas and practices within current structures, which themselves are subject to change.

Cultures are externally affected via contact between societies, which may also produce—or inhibit—social shifts and changes in cultural practices. War or competition over resources may impact technological development or social dynamics. Cultural traits often cross social boundaries and diffuse among many different societies and are thus an important mechanism of change.

There are several elements that together constitute the culture of a particular region or the culture of particular people. They include language, norms (such as folkways, mores, taboos, and rituals), values (entities of value for a culture), religion and beliefs, social collectives (social groupings, organizations, communities, institutions, societies), and social roles. Cultural anthropologists take seriously the relationship between a culture and its environment to explain different aspects of a culture. But most modern cultural anthropologists have adopted a general systems approach, examining cultures as emergent systems, and argue that one must consider the whole social environment, which includes political and economic relations among cultures. There are still others who continue to reject the entirety of the evolutionary thinking and look instead at historical contingencies, contacts with other cultures, and the operation of cultural symbol systems. As a result, the simplistic notion of cultural evolution has grown less useful and given way to an entire series of more nuanced approaches to the relationship of culture and environment.

Today, the theory of cultural evolution is an underpinning for other, more complex explanations for cultural change, and for the most part archaeologists believe social changes are not only driven by biology or a strict adaptation to change but by a complex web of social, environmental, and biological factors. Cultures around the world are undergoing change due to environmental stresses, such as climate change. Globalization and increased consumerism are increasing environmental stress by contributing to deforestation. Additionally, other stresses such as the introduction of foreign species, pollution, and urban sprawl affect cultural evolution.

Technological innovations can enhance, displace, or devalue human existence and culture. Advances in medical technology have contributed to demographic changes, including increased longevity and decreasing fertility. For example, although China has slowed its population increases through a one-child per family policy, the median age of its people will soar in the next thirty-five years. "Western" or European culture began to undergo rapid change starting with the arrival of Columbus in the New World, and continuing with the industrial revolution. The Modern Period, from 1914–1945, is characterized as a highly transformative era, with World War I serving as the watershed moment initiating and forever marking the Modern period.

All cultures are inherently predisposed to change and, at the same time, to resist change. There are dynamic processes operating that encourage the acceptance of new ideas and things while there are others that encourage changeless stability. It is likely that social and psychological chaos would result if there were not the conservative forces resisting change. There are three general sources of influence or pressure that are responsible for both change and resistance to it: forces at work within a society, contact between societies, and changes in the natural environment.

Within a society, processes leading to change include invention and culture loss. Inventions may be either technological or ideological. The latter includes such things as the invention of algebra and calculus or the creation of a representative parliament as a replacement for rule by royal decree. Technological inventions include new tools, energy sources, and transportation methods as well as more frivolous and ephemeral things such as style of dress and bodily adornment. Culture loss is an inevitable result of old cultural patterns being replaced by new ones. For instance, not many Americans today know how to care for a horse. A century ago, this was common knowledge, except in a few large urban centers. Since then, vehicles with internal combustion engines have replaced horses as our primary means of transportation and horse care knowledge lost its importance. As a result, children are rarely taught these skills. Instead, they are trained in the use of the new technologies of automobiles, televisions, stereos, cellular phones, computers, and iPods.

Within a society, processes that result in the resistance to change include habit and the integration of culture traits. Older people, in particular, are often reticent to replace their comfortable, long familiar cultural patterns. Habitual behavior provides emotional security in a threatening world of change. Religion also often provides strong moral justification and support for maintaining traditional ways. In the early twenty-first century, this is especially true of nations mostly guided by Islamic Law, such as Iran, Saudi Arabia, Afghanistan, and Pakistan.

The fact that cultural institutions are integrated and often interdependent is a major source of resistance to change. For instance, in the second half of the twentieth century, rapidly changing roles of North American and European women were resisted by many men because it inevitably resulted in changes in their roles as well. Male and female roles do not exist independent of each other. This sort of integration of cultural traits inevitably slows down and modifies cultural changes. Needless to say, it is a source of frustration for both those who want to change and those who do not.

The processes leading to change that occur as a result of contact between societies are diffusion, acculturation, and transculturation. Diffusion is the movement of things and ideas from one culture to another. When diffusion occurs, the form of a trait may move from one society to another. For instance, when McDonald's first brought their American style hamburgers to Moscow and Beijing, they were accepted as luxury foods for special occasions because they were relatively expensive and exotic. In America, of course, they have a very different meaning—they are ordinary every day fast food items.

Acculturation is what happens to an entire culture when alien traits diffuse on a large scale and substantially replace traditional cultural patterns. After several centuries of relentless pressure from European Americans to adopt their ways, Native American cultures have been largely acculturated. As a result, the vast majority of American Indians now speak English instead of their ancestral language, wear European style clothes, go to school to learn about the world from a European perspective, and see themselves as being a part of the broader American society. As Native American societies continue to acculturate, most are experiencing a corresponding loss of their traditional cultures despite efforts of preservationists in their communities.

While acculturation is what happens to an entire culture when alien traits overwhelm it, transculturation is what happens to an individual when he or she moves to another society and adopts its culture. Immigrants who successfully learn the language and accept as their own the cultural patterns of their adopted country have transculturated. In contrast, people who live as socially isolated expatriates in a foreign land for years without desiring or expecting to become assimilated participants in the host culture are not transculturating.

There is one last process leading to change that occurs as an invention within a society as a result of an idea that diffuses from another. This is stimulus diffusion—a genuine invention that is sparked by an idea from another culture. It is likely that Ancient Egyptians around 3050 BC invented their hieroglyphic writing system after learning about the cuneiform writing system invented by Sumerians in what is today Southern Iraq. There are processes operating in the contact between cultures as well that result in resistance to change. These are due to "us versus them" competitive feelings and perceptions. Ethnocentrism also leads people to reject alien ideas and things as being unnatural and even immoral. These ingroup-outgroup dynamics commonly result in resistance to acculturation and assimilation.

One of the main forces today in cultural change is technology. Today we live in a world that some might argue is overrun with technology. As a result, the jobs we do, how we learn, the structure of our family and social relationships, what we eat, and so much more is shifting rapidly. Technology, especially the Internet, has played a role in this change. Peoples lived in isolated communities for thousands of years, but in today's world we can be connected through technology to anyone anywhere in the world. With modern air transportation people can travel to anywhere in the world in just a few hours. The pattern of migration since the beginning of the twentieth century has left many with the difficult reality of not knowing exactly where their own ancestors came from, what cultural traditions they practiced, and which languages their people spoke. Thankfully, genetic research is now allowing people to reconstruct the trail of long lost migrations.

The downside of modern technology is that we are drifting toward a more homogeneous world. We are in danger of losing ancient skills, visionary wisdom, and many languages. At the moment we humans speak something on the order of 6,500 languages. If we look at the number of languages we will likely pass on to our children, that number is 600. The vast majority of these languages are oral and never written down. A wealth of traditional wisdom is found in oral history, poetry, epic tales, creation stories, riddles, and wise sayings. Much of what humans have learned over the millennia about how to thrive on this planet is encapsulated in threatened languages. We are currently in the middle of a massive extinction of the world's languages as cultures abandon indigenous tongues for global megalanguages. Global language extinction threatens to disrupt oral traditions as never before, risking the wholesale loss of an enormous and ancient accretion of knowledge, preserved for centuries in the world's oral traditions. They exist only in memory. When languages vanish, we lose unique human knowledge. When ideas go extinct, we all grow poorer.

Respect for the value and importance of cultural diversity is one of the great challenges of our age. Cultures and ethnicities matter. They provide the vital constraints of tradition and comfort that allow civilizations to exist. To celebrate our differences is a wonderful part of being human. Learning new languages and traveling to other places are universal curiosities, uniting people in a way that underscores the fact that our own DNA is 99.9% identical to that of everybody else on this planet. We must remember that with the multiplicity of cultures and ethnicities, we are all one.

**Sistine Chapel ceiling, painted by Michelangelo between 1508 and 1512, at the commission of Pope Julius II.**

# CHAPTER 4

## Evolution: Religions

Religion has been defined in a wide variety of ways. Sociologists and anthropologists tend to see religion as an abstract set of ideas, values, or experiences developed as part of a cultural matrix. Others define religion as any specific system of beliefs about deity, often involving rituals, a code of ethics, and a philosophy of life. For better and for worse, religion has been a major influence on human behavior, culture, and events throughout time. Like so many other aspects of life, religion is a complicated phenomenon, at times bound up with the best in human thought and behavior and at other times, bound up with the worst. The evolution of religion is the story of mankind, with saints and sinners, war and peace, tragedy and ecstasy. Nothing else has had such an impact on culture, politics, and ethics.

During early human existence belief in the supernatural fulfilled several important functions—it explained their origins, provided a feeling of connection with the universe, provided a purpose for their existence, led to establishing a moral code, fostered a sense of community, and provided a sense of connection with the supernatural. The roots of religion lie in humanity's quest to comprehend the world and our place within it.

It is likely that religion helped early humans evolve from primates dominated by short term instincts into human beings capable of forming sophisticated societies. With growing powers of deduction, while possessing limited information, it probably seemed logical to primitive humans that the environment was controlled by beings like themselves but with much greater powers. These beings were the gods and goddesses of the time. They appeared to have the power to grant or withhold the necessities of life, and so it was reasonable to assume that they created us, and as their children we owed them the same respect that we expected from our children. That led to the worship of these gods and goddesses.

One can only speculate about early beliefs. Stone Age people probably believed they were living at the center of the universe. Their universe was relatively small. They probably believed that all movement was a product of will, and will was spirit. They saw their world as having many spirits. These spirits were gods to them. As such, they were polytheists believing in many spirits or gods. When ancient cave painters drew animals, they may have believed that such an animal would appear and success in a hunt would occur. Not knowing how things worked, Stone Age people attributed many things to the magic of the spirits. When a person saw his reflection in the water he may well have believed he was seeing his own spirit. Lightning, rain, the tides, and procreation were magic. Fire must have seemed like magic, and it was spirit as it danced around. Stone Age people likely saw everything in nature as spirit and they respected the many forms. Thunder, lightning, strong winds, floods were anger. People feared the anger of the spirits and hoped to placate them with words, gifts, and rituals. People began to explain elements of the world that they could not understand by telling stories about the actions of gods and goddesses. These stories reflected the environments from which they emerged and evolved to embody the core values and beliefs of the people.

Religious beliefs are found in virtually every society throughout human history. Many traditions held magicians or witchdoctors as essential to any contact with the gods and goddesses. People had to have these sorcerers within their most sacred ceremonies. The sorcerers in those traditions were essential to creation and to birth. The exact nature of the first religions is lost in prehistory. In looking at later undeveloped faiths, it is likely that the first religious beliefs combined elements of magic with rites of supplication and invocation, possibly involving dancing and chanting. Such rituals were intended to help worshipers leave the confines of their own existence to come into contact with a more universal, supernatural level of being. Individuals felt to be particularly adept at communicating with the spirit world acted as intermediaries between worshipers and their gods. These intermediaries became guardians of ritual and often arbiters of acceptable and unacceptable behavior. Meeting places or sites of worship became more regular such as a hilltop or specific landmark. Eventually buildings were constructed to house artifacts and images sacred to a deity or deities. People explained elements of the world that they could not understand by telling stories about the actions of gods and goddesses. These stories mutated as cultures connected and their religions evolved. The stories reflected the environments from which they emerged and came to embody the core values and beliefs of the civilization.

Rules in earliest human societies were created through discussion. There were no written laws or holy books from which to take guidance. No one presumed to be above others in authority. No one exhorted the group about laws laid down by any of the spirits whose presence they felt. There were no preachers or priests, but there were shamans (witchdoctors). In Stone Age societies almost anyone could be a shaman. They probably claimed to be in communication with spirits, but, rather than command, the shamans most likely merely described or suggested, and performed what they and others imagined were cures. One can imagine that shamans strutted, danced, and made shouting noises in an attempt to display their powers. Many perhaps helped themselves to visions by using hallucinogenic drugs, perhaps from the bark of a tree. From what has been learned about Stone Age societies, it appears that in general individuals did not pray for themselves. Their work and their prayers were community endeavors. Their relationship with their gods was as a group. Individuals identified their welfare with the welfare of the group, and morality was what they found to be best for the group.

During the time of ancient Mesopotamia, beginning at about 3500 BC, the facts of nature were attributed to the workings of divine forces. Thus, there were many gods and goddesses, including four creator gods who were themselves created by the forces of Taimat and Abzu, who had emerged from a primordial chaos of water. The highest of the four gods was the sky-god An. After An came Enhil who could either produce raging storms or act to help man. Ninkhursag was the earth goddess. The fourth god was Enki, the water god and patron of wisdom. These four gods did not act alone, but consulted with an assembly of fifty— the Annunaki. In addition to these gods and goddesses, the world was populated with innumerable spirits and demons. The ancient Mesopotamia gods bound people together in their social groups and provided what they needed to survive. It was believed the gods could be prevailed upon if ceremonies were performed to their liking, and so a priestly class developed.

All early religions were polytheistic. Their followers believed in and worshiped multiple gods or deities. A religion's gods or deities together formed a pantheon. Well-known historical polytheistic pantheons included the Sumerian gods and the Egyptian gods, and the classical attested pantheon which included the Ancient Greek religion, and Roman religion. Post classical polytheistic religions include Norse gods Aesir and Vanir, the Yoruba Orisha, the Aztec gods, Maya gods, and many others. Religions have evolved over the centuries and those that have survived have done so in a constant state of change as the world has changed.

Today, most historical polytheistic religions are negatively referred to as mythology. In many civilizations, pantheons tended to grow over time. Deities first worshipped as the patrons of cities or places eventually came to be collected together as empires extended over larger territories. Conquests could lead to the subordination of the elder culture's pantheon to a newer one, as in the Greek Titanomachia, and possibly also in the case of the Aesir and Vanir in the Norse religions. Cultural exchanges often led to a deity being renowned in different places under different names, as with the Greeks, Etruscans, and Romans, and also to the introduction of elements of a "foreign" religion into a local cult, as with Egyptian Osiris worship brought to ancient Greece. The

Greek god Zeus (the father of all gods in the Greek pantheon) later became the Roman god Jupiter (the sky god), and the Greek god Ares (the god of war) later became the Roman god Mars. Other major Roman gods include Juno (the patron goddess of all women), Minerva (wisdom, crafts, and industries), Venus (beauty and love), Vulcan (fire), Vesta (hearth and home), Mercury (merchants), and Janus (the two-headed god of doorways). The Romans also had many other lesser gods. Every home had its own group of household spirits. When Rome became an empire, emperors were also considered to be divine; some emperors were worshiped as gods even while they were still alive. In the Nile Valley, the myths of the ancient Egyptians told of animal-headed deities who controlled various aspects of life and furthermore presided over the afterlife. For the Greeks, their gods lived high on Mount Olympus and resembled their own aristocratic rulers who were flush with power and given to self-indulgence, feuding, deception, and petty jealousies. The Greeks lived in fear of offending the gods and goddesses and in suffering their anger. Natural processes that were not fully understood were explained as the work of supernatural beings.

In the ancient Near East, each city had a local patron deity, such as Shamash at Larsa, or Sin at Ur. The first claims of global supremacy of a specific god date to the Late Bronze Age (circa 600 BC), with Akhenaton's *Great Hymn to the Aton*. Currents of monotheism emerged in Vedic India in the same time period. Philosophical monotheism and the associated concept of absolute good and evil emerged around 500 BC in the cultures of Greece and Rome, notably with Plato, elaborated into the idea of *The One in Neo-Platonism*. Monotheistic ideas of Judaism and Platonic Idealism emerged during the second and third centuries BC, and the fourth to sixth century AD gave rise to Christian theology. The major and basic source of monotheism is the narrative of the Hebrew Bible, the source of Judaism. The first of the three parts of the Hebrew Bible is based largely on the Torah which according to Jewish tradition was revealed to Moses in 1312 BC on Mount Sinai. Today, the majority of scholars agree that the Torah does not have a single author, and that its composition took place over centuries. The Torah is divided into five books, with names in

English of Genesis, Exodus, Leviticus, Numbers, and Deuteronomy. Judaism probably also received influences from various non-biblical religions present in Egypt and Syria. This can be seen by the Torah's reference to Egyptian culture in Genesis and the story of Moses, as well as the mention of Hittite and Hurrian cultures of Syria in the Genesis story of Abraham.

In traditional Jewish thought, which provided the basis of the Christian and Islamic religions, monotheism was regarded as its most basic belief. Judaism and Islam have traditionally interpreted scriptures as exclusive monotheism, while Christianity diverted to a more complex form of tripartite monotheism as a result of attributing divinity to Jesus, a Judean Jew, in the first century AD and later defining him as the physical son of God.

The religion of Zoroastrianism was founded by Zoroaster (Zarathushtra) who was born among the religious elite in northeastern Iran. He became a priest in the local polytheistic faith of his time, but grew disillusioned with the rigid and oppressive caste system that it perpetuated. His life changed after a vision of Ahura Mazda, the divine creator. He then founded a monotheistic religion that emerged in Iran around 1500 BC. Perhaps Zoroastrianism's monotheistic belief influenced early Torah. It is believed that Zoroaster traveled to southern Iran, where he gathered many followers. The religion was common throughout Iran by the fifth century BC. In 331 BC, Alexander the Great conquered Mesopotamia, and within two years seized all the lands of the Persian Empire. The Zoroastrian priests were slaughtered by the troops and much of the oral doctrine was lost. Zoroastrianism exists today as a minority religion in Iran and India.

The indigenous religious beliefs and practices of the ancient Maya focused on various interlocking cyclical periods of time, such as the 260-day Tzolkin calendar. Also notable are the cardinal directions and individual associations with "nahuals" or external souls in animal form. Their rituals and ceremonies were very closely associated with hundreds of celestial and terrestrial cycles which they observed and inscribed as separate calendars. The Maya priests had the job of interpreting these cycles and giving a prophetic outlook on the future based on the number relations of all their calendars. If the interpretations of the priests spelled bad times to come, sacrifices would be performed to please the gods. Sacrifices might be small animals like chickens, or "bloodletting" by high officials, and sometimes included human sacrifices. They would engage in rituals such as cutting their own ears, tongues, and penises with the intention of satisfying the gods.

It is known that the Maya believed that the cosmos has three major planes, the sky, the earth, and the underworld. Heaven was thought to have thirteen different layers or levels where various gods dwelt. The underworld, which was called Xibalbá, was believed to be divided into nine layers which were inhabited by the aged Maya gods of death and putrefaction. The Maya believed that Xibalbá was the final resting place of souls after death, and that the deities of the underworld would torment anyone there. The Sun and Itzamna, both aged gods, dominated the Maya idea of the sky. The night sky was considered a window showing all supernatural doings. The Maya configured constellations of gods and places, saw the unfolding of narratives in their seasonal movements, and believed that the intersection of all possible worlds was in the night sky.

There is a massive array of Maya gods and supernatural characters in the Maya religious tradition only some of which recur with regularity. Most of them have both good and evil traits, and are often revered for both. What is inappropriate during one season might come to pass in another since much of the Maya religious tradition is based on cycles and not permanence. The lifecycle of maize (corn) lies at the heart of Maya belief. This philosophy is demonstrated on the Maya belief in the maize god as a central religious figure. The Maya bodily ideal is also based on the form of the young maize god, which is demonstrated in their artwork. The maize god was also a model of courtly life for the classical Maya. The Maya believed that the date on which a person was born determined their fate throughout life. Philosophically, the Maya believed that knowing the past meant knowing the cyclical influences that create the present, and by knowing the influences of the present one could foretell the cyclical influences in the future.

Modern Maya religion is strongly influenced by Catholicism. Today's modern Maya do not consider themselves polytheists.

However, much of their religious practice centers on the observation of the Tzolkin 260-day calendar. On special occasions, a wide variety of aromatic substances are burned in a central fire at a traditional outdoor altar site, and a Maya priest invokes and prays to entities such as the 260 days; the cardinal directions; the ancestors of those present; important Maya towns, lakes, caves, or volcanoes; and deities from the Popol Vuh. The Popol Vuh is a body of myth and historical narratives of the post classic Quiché kingdom in Guatemala's western highlands. It is the creation story of the Maya.

The Maya believe all of nature—the trees, the rivers, the animals—possess spirits that must be respected and appeased. Humans are part of nature and must be humble and reverent. The balance between the spirit and physical world is maintained through scrupulous observance of traditions such as youth initiation, the formal rituals which lead to marriage, service in the community religious and civil hierarchy, and most importantly by frequent performance of ceremonies to invoke and appease the Maya spirits. These ceremonies are performed in accordance with the 260-day Tzolkin calendar and also at times during the year which correspond to the stages in the cultivation of the maize crop: clearing the land, planting, and harvesting. Maize to the Maya is sacred above all other crops.

Today Hinduism, Buddhism, Judaism, Christianity, and Islam account for close to 6 billion of the world's 7 billion people. Regardless of all the differences between their beliefs, they all seek the same fulfillment from their religious experience: a feeling of connection with the universe, an understanding of their purpose, a moral code, a sense of fellowship, and a sense of the supernatural. Human yearning has inspired many different forms of faith numbering in the thousands, from the myths of the ancient Egyptians to short-lived storefront churches. The majority of the world's faiths have disappeared, and those that survive today have done so in a constant state of change, as the world itself has changed. Scriptures have undergone review and reinterpretation. Visionary individuals have changed the direction of many churches. Political events have dragged faiths into visceral violence and bitterness. Churches have split and formed splinter congregations. It is the enduring power of belief and the optimism and comfort it offers that draws people to the various religions. While religion over the ages has often been something to kill for, it has far more often been something to live for. For most people faith is the framework that provides a semblance of sense to their lives.

## Hinduism

The oldest of today's religions, Hinduism, emerged between 2600 and 1500 BC. There are many gods. The three major Hindu gods are Brahma, Vishnu, and Shiva. Owing to its vastness and richness, the origin of this ancient way of life, cannot be ascribed to a single founder or a single time. The phrase "Hinduism" is obtained from Sindhu—a mighty river flowing in the ancient Indus Valley of India. Folklore states that the inhabitants of the valley were termed Hindus as they dwelled in the Sindhu (Indus) Valley. The earliest sacred writings from which Hinduism emerged were based on four texts that originated in the Indus Valley. These texts, known collectively as *Vedas* (knowledge), evolved over a period of almost a thousand years between 1400 and 400 BC into their present written form. The oldest of the four texts is the *Rig Veda* comprising more than 1,000 verses written in Sanskrit. Two of the later Vedas describe the ceremonies and practices of the Vedic religion. The forth Veda, *Upanishads*, is the basis for much of Hinduism today. It is in the *Upanishads* that first stated each person possesses a soul or spirit which cannot be destroyed.

## Buddhism

Buddhism is based on the life of Siddhartha Gautama, who lived in the Himalayan foothills of northern India. Legend has it that he was a young prince kept in isolation from the ills of the world. With curiosity growing, he went out alone into the city and was shocked by what he saw. At some point he left his home and family to wander as a beggar looking for enlightenment spending six years in poverty. Realizing that to find enlightenment he would have to look inside himself, he sat down beneath a tree, resolved not to move until he had attained spiritual ecstasy. Three nights later he stood up and resumed his journey. He had become the Buddha. For over forty years he wandered through northern

India spreading the injunction "Cease to do evil; learn to do good, and purify your heart." Like other Indian thinkers of his time, he believed the dead were reincarnated innumerable times in different human or even animal forms, rising and falling in status according to how well they had lived their previous lives.

Buddhism remained a minority creed until about 259 BC, when it was taken up by Asoka, India's Mauryan ruler, and thus became the official religion throughout most of India. Buddhism was particularly popular among the merchants of the thriving cities. These merchants were part of an extensive international trade network such that Buddhism spread along the trade routes. Missionaries were sent to the Island of Sri Lanka and to Southeast Asia and later to China, Korea, Japan, and Indonesia, where the message proved more enduring than in its Indian birthplace. Today Buddhism is the most important organized religion in China. Its practice has been adapted to incorporate the basic tenets of Confucianism and Taoism, such as ancestor worship, creating a religion that is uniquely appropriate to Chinese culture.

## Shintoism

Shintoism is Japan's major religion. Its origins date back to the arrival of Buddhism in Japan in 538 A.D., when followers of indigenous nature and fertility religions set about formalizing their belief system to distinguish it from Buddhism. At the heart of Shinto are *kami,* which are sacred spirits that exist in everything. The kami came to be seen as abstract "spirituality" embodied in forms such as the wind, rain, trees, rivers, and mountains. People also become kami after they die, so ancestor worship is a significant factor of Shinto.

## Judaism

Judaism claims a historical continuity spanning more than 3000 years. It is one of the oldest monotheistic religions. The Hebrew Bible, the source of Judaism, was formed from a collection of texts created from the tenth century BC to the second century BC. Judaism is a faith which recognizes Abraham as a Patriarch. Judaism's texts, traditions, and values play a major role in later Abrahamic religions, including Christianity, Islam, and the

Baha'i faith. Many aspects of Judaism have also directly or indirectly influenced secular Western ethics and civil law.

According to traditional Rabbinic Judaism, God revealed his laws and commandments to Moses on Mount Sinai in the form of both the written and oral Torah. The largest Jewish religious movements are Orthodox Judaism, Conservative Judaism, and Reform Judaism. A major source of difference between these groups is their approach to Jewish law. Orthodox Judaism maintains that the Torah and Jewish law are divine in origin, eternal, and unalterable, and that they should be strictly followed. Conservative and Reform Judaism are more liberal, with Conservative Judaism generally promoting a more traditional interpretation of Judaism's requirements than Reform Judaism. A typical Reform position is that Jewish law should be viewed as a set of general guidelines rather than as a set of restrictions and obligations whose observance is required of all Jews. Historically, special courts enforced Jewish law; today, these courts still exist but the practice of Judaism is mostly voluntary. Authority on theological and legal matters is not vested in any one person or organization, but in the sacred texts and the many rabbis and scholars who interpret these texts.

In modern times, Judaism lacks a centralized authority that would dictate an exact religious dogma. Because of this, many different variations on the basic beliefs are considered within the scope of Judaism. Even so, all Jewish religious movements are, to a greater or lesser extent, based on the principles of the Hebrew Bible and on various commentaries such as the Talmud and Midrash. Judaism also universally recognizes the Biblical Covenant between God and the Patriarch Abraham as well as the additional aspects of the Covenant revealed to Moses, who is considered Judaism's greatest prophet.

## Christianity

Christianity began as a Jewish sect in the mid-first century. Originating in the eastern Mediterranean, it quickly grew in size and influence over a few decades, and by the fourth century had become the dominant religion within the Roman Empire. Christians believe that Jesus is the Messiah prophesied in the

Hebrew Bible, referred to as the "Old Testament" in Christianity. Jesus emerged as a preacher and leader during a time of great popular discontent, as various peoples of Judaea resented Roman rule. He was an impressive speaker, with a gift for telling parables (educational stories). Of all the prophets, he is the only one who claimed to be the son of God. After Jesus' death, Christianity grew apart from Judaism and was carried by the Apostles throughout the Roman Empire. In the Middle Eastern heartlands of Christianity, the teachings of Jesus followed a long tradition of prophets who preached a special bond between their one god, Yahweh, and the Jews.

Christianity was just one religion among a number of eastern cults popular among the Romans. Its assertion that there were no gods beyond the Christian God brought persecution from authorities with a vested interest in maintaining pagan beliefs. In the first centuries AD, the followers of Christ evolved from a loose band of disciples into tight-knit communities of worship. Through the persistence and faith of early Christians and through the conversion of the Emperor Constantine in 312 AD, Christianity became more accepted and grew in its followers. This shift affected Christian believers as the church went from being a persecuted minority to a privileged minority. Freed from Roman persecution, Christianity underwent an institutional revolution, developing an organizational structure and unified doctrine still recognizable into today's Catholic Church. The Catholic Church is the oldest continuously active organization on Earth and one of the most influential institutions in the world.

An influence on Christian theology was Manichaeanism, a religion founded by the Parthian prophet Mani in the early third century AD in Mesopotamia. It was based on dualism, or the doctrine of opposing principles: light and darkness, good and evil. Light was good and associated with god, while dark was evil and associated with matter. Christianity also proposes a dualistic view of good and evil. Manichaeanism thrived until the seventh century, and at one point was practiced as far apart as China and the Roman Empire. The religion disappeared after the fourteenth century.

Christianity is based on the life and teachings of Jesus of Nazareth as presented in the canonical gospels (the writings of Matthew, Mark, Luke, and John) and other New Testament writings. The gospels of Matthew, Mark, and Luke are known as the synoptic gospels because they include many of the same stories, often in the same sequence, and sometimes exactly the same wording. The degree of parallelism in content, narrative arrangement, language, and sentence structures can only be accounted for by literary interdependence. Most scholars believe that these gospels share the same point of view and are clearly linked. The canonical gospels of John written fifteen to twenty years later differ greatly from the gospels of Matthew, Mark, and Luke. Estimates for the dates when the canonical gospel accounts were written vary significantly, and the evidence for any of the dates is scanty. Because the earliest surviving complete copies of the gospels date to the 4th century and because only fragments and quotations exist before that, scholars use higher criticism to propose likely ranges of dates for the original gospel writings. Scholars variously assess the majority view of when the canonical gospels were written as follows: Mark (circa 68–73), Matthew (circa 70–100), Luke (circa 80–100), and John (circa 90-110). By these assessments they were written in the timeframe of thirty to eighty years after the death of Jesus. In differentiating history from invention, historians interpret the gospel accounts skeptically but generally regard the synoptic gospels as including significant amounts of historically reliable information about Jesus.

Mainstream Christianity teaches Jesus is the son of God, God having become human and the savior of humanity. Because of this, Christians commonly refer to Jesus as Christ or Messiah. The three largest groups in the world of Christianity are the Roman Catholic Church, the Eastern Orthodox churches, and the various churches of Protestantism. The Roman Catholic and Eastern Orthodox patriarchates split from one another in the East-West Schism of 1054 AD, and Protestantism came into existence during the Protestant Reformation of the sixteenth century, splitting from the Roman Catholic Church.

## Islam

The founder of the Islamic faith was the prophet Muhammad. He was born in Mecca, Arabia, in 570. His father died before he was born, and his mother died while he was a child. He was raised mainly by his uncle, Abu Hamza. He became a successful merchant and at the age of twenty-five married Khadijah, a wealthy woman several years his senior. In 610, he began seeing visions. In the years that followed he had several visions of the angel Gabriel dictating to him the word of Allah—God. With religious zeal and a message of charity for the poor, Muhammad and his followers quickly found themselves at odds with Mecca's wealthy elite, and in 622 they fled for the neighboring city of Medina. After the death of Khadijah he took multiple wives, often to cement alliances with other local tribal leaders. He also became a military leader, organizing a Muslim army that defended Medina against attacks by the Meccans. In time the Muslims gained control of Mecca. This marked the start of conquests such that by the time he died in 632, the Arabs had already carried the word of Islam through much of West Asia by both force of arms and by inspiration. Within a few centuries his group of followers spread from the deserts of the Arabian Peninsula to create an empire that covered much of the Middle East, North Africa, and West Asia. Soon after Muhammad's death Islam itself split over who succeeded Muhammad as leader of the faith into Sunnis and Shiites. To this day this division often causes problems between the two groups. Two smaller sects of Islam are Ahmadiyya and Druze.

Islam belongs to the same tradition as Judaism and Christianity in that all three are monotheistic, all three acknowledge Abraham as a patriarchal figure, and Islam recognizes the divinity of Jesus; however, it considers Jesus as just one of God's prophets rather than his son. Islam maintains a strong political influence and has the determination and military experience to impose itself on its neighbors. Muslims do not view Muhammad as the creator of Islam but instead regard him as the last messenger of God, through which the Qur'an, the religious text of Islam, was revealed. Muslims view Muhammad as the restorer of the original, uncorrupted monotheistic faith of Adam, Abraham, Moses, Jesus, and other prophets. In Muslim tradition,

Muhammad is viewed as the last and the greatest in a series of prophets—as the man closest to perfection, the possessor of all virtues. For the last twenty-two years of his life, beginning at age forty in 610, Muhammad supposedly started receiving revelations from God. The content of these revelations, known as the Qur'an, was dictated by Muhammad, and memorized and recorded by his companions.

## Confucianism

Confucianism is a Chinese ethical and philosophical system developed from the teachings of the Chinese philosopher Confucius (551–478 BC). While it is not recognized by most people as a religion, as many as 1.5 billion people follow Confucian ideals. It is a complex system of moral, social, political, philosophical, and quasi-religious thought that influenced the culture and history of East Asia. It might be considered a state religion of some East Asian countries, because of state promotion of Confucian philosophies. Cultures and countries strongly influenced by Confucianism include mainland China, Taiwan, Korea, Japan, and Vietnam, as well as various territories settled predominantly by Chinese people, such as Singapore. In Confucianism, human beings are teachable, improvable and perfectible through personal and communal endeavor especially including self-cultivation and self-creation.

A main idea of Confucianism is the cultivation of virtue and the development of moral perfection. Confucianism holds that one should give up one's life, if necessary, either passively or actively, for the sake of upholding the cardinal moral values. Although Confucianism is often followed in a religious manner by the Chinese, arguments continue over whether it is a religion. Confucianism discusses elements of the afterlife and views concerning Heaven, but it is relatively unconcerned with some spiritual matters often considered essential to religious thought, such as the nature of the soul.

Confucius, Buddha, Jesus, and Muhammad were four extraordinary sages who influenced world civilizations more deeply than any other human beings in history. They were all born into ancient cultures in the midst of tumultuous changes. Each addressed fundamental existential problems within their societies, developing codes of ethics and behavior that broke with the past, and offering bold new visions of human life. Four centuries after the rise of the scientific worldview, their influence in human affairs continues to be fundamental, underscoring issues ranging from questions of ethics and justice to religious and political conflicts to other issues that dominate today's headlines. In the twenty-first century, much of humanity still looks to the lives, teachings, and actions of these four men for guidance on how to live, for their conceptions of morality, and for understanding the most crucial human values. As models of human living they remain dynamically alive for countless billions of people around the world, exemplifying the moral and spiritual precepts our civilizations are built on. Their influence extends over most of the human population.

Many detailed books have been written discussing Hinduism, Buddhism, Judaism, Christianity, and Islam. Religions have had a vital impact upon human behavior, cultures, and political events throughout history. The above paragraphs are but a cursory glance to show how diverse faiths have evolved. Hinduism evolved over a period of 1,000 years having multiple gods. Buddhism owes its origin to the spiritual enlightenment of Siddhartha Gautama who became the Buddha. Judaism, Christianity, and Islam owe their origins to the visions of prophets. In spirituality, visions comprise inspirational renderings, generally of a future state and/or of a supernatural being and are believed by followers of certain religions to come from a deity, sometimes directly or indirectly via prophets, and serve to inspire or prod believers as part of a revelation or an epiphany. Visions generally have more clarity than dreams, but traditionally fewer psychological connotations. The psychological mechanism to engender visionary perception and trance phenomena is focused intention and attention. A vision in the context of spirituality does not necessarily mean the actual appearance of an entity. With respect to religions, the prophets were persons with focused intention and attention who professed their visions. They are individuals who claim to have been in contact with the supernatural or the divine, and serve as intermediaries with humanity, delivering newfound knowledge from the supernatural entity to other people. Moses, Abraham, Muhammad, and Jesus, among others, are considered as prophets.

Claims of prophets have existed in many cultures through history, including Judaism, Christianity, Islam, the Sybilline, Delphic Oracles practices in Ancient Greece, Zoroaster, the Völuspá in Old Norse, and many others. Traditionally, prophets are regarded as having a role in society that promotes change due to their messages and actions. The prophets certainly had good intensions; however one must view their claims as to having had contact with the divine or supernatural with some skepticism. They always seem to have gone up on a mountain or into a dessert or some other spot alone for some period of time and then returned with their messages. The messages are not necessarily consistent from one prophet to the next and often adapted to fit the times. The messages are typically good and ones those individuals could deduce with some focused intention and attention.

Claims by prophets in themselves do not prove the existence of God. Believing that God exists is based on faith. A basic problem is that there is no universally accepted definition of God. Today in the West, the term "God" typically refers to a monotheistic concept of a supreme being that possesses every possible perfection, including such qualities as omniscience, omnipotence, and perfect benevolence. Other philosophical approaches take a logically simple definition of God such as "the Prime Mover" or "the Uncaused Cause" or "the Ultimate Creator" or "a being greater than which nothing can be conceived." As we have seen, mankind's concept of God has evolved. Since God is neither an entity in our universe nor a mathematical object it is not obvious what kind of arguments or proofs are relevant to God's existence. There is to date no conclusive scientific proof of the existence, or non-existence, of God. Science has destroyed some of the dogmas of faith, by providing alternative explanations that are impossible to deny. Geology and evolution have explained away most of the creation myths of religions; while history and psychology have attacked religion by casting doubt on its very origins. A belief in God is strictly a matter of faith. Theism is the proposition that God exists. Atheism is the view that God does not exist. Agnosticism is the view that whether or not God exists is unknown or unknowable.

A negative view as to the existence of God was presented by the atheist Robert Green Ingersoll in 1872. Following are the fist couple of paragraphs of his dissertation:

*Each nation has created a god, and the god has always resembled his creators. He hated and loved what they hated and loved, and he was invariably found on the side of those in power. Each god was intensely patriotic, and detested all nations but his own. All these gods demanded praise, flattery, and worship. Most of them were pleased with sacrifice, and the smell of innocent blood has ever been considered a divine perfume. All these gods have insisted upon having a vast number of priests, and the priests have always insisted upon being supported by the people, and the principal business of these priests has been to boast about their god, and to insist that he could easily vanquish all the other gods put together.*

*These gods have been manufactured after numberless models, and according to the most grotesque fashions. Some have had a thousand arms, some a hundred heads, some are adorned with necklaces of living snakes, some are armed with clubs, some with sword and shield, some with bucklers, and some have wings as a cherub; some were invisible, some would show themselves entire, and some would only show their backs; some were jealous, some were foolish, some turned themselves into men, some into swans, some into bulls, some into doves, and some into Holy Ghosts, and made love to the beautiful daughters of men. Some were married – all ought to have been – and some were considered as old bachelors from all eternity. Some had children, and the children were turned into gods and worshiped as their fathers had been. Most of these gods were revengeful, savage, lustful, and ignorant. As they generally depended upon their priests for information, their ignorance can hardly excite our astonishment.*

Aristotle wrote: *"Men create gods after their own image."*

Mark Twain's frankest views on religion appeared in his final autobiography, which was not to be published until 100 years after his death. He died in 1909. His autobiography was published in November of 2010. In it he said:

*There is one notable thing about our Christianity: bad, bloody, merciless, money-grabbing, and predatory. The invention of hell measured by our Christianity of today, bad as it is, hypocritical as it is, empty and hollow as it is, neither the deity nor his son is a Christian, nor qualified for that moderately high place. Ours is a terrible religion. The fleets of the world could swim in spacious comfort in the innocent blood it has spilled.*

In an interview, theoretical physicist Stephen Hawking stated there is a fundamental difference between religion, which is based on authority, and science, which is based on observation and reason. In *Grand Design,* 2010, the physicist declared that it was "not necessary to invoke God ... to get the universe going." He has maintained this position since very early in his career, telling German newsmagazine Der Speigel in 1988 that "what I have done is to show that it is possible for the way the universe began to be determined by the laws of science. In that case, it would not be necessary to appeal to God to decide how the universe began." "This doesn't prove that there is no God, only that God is not necessary," he said.

Pope Benedict said something like this: "The Big Bang theory is proof that God exists." Actually it's not. It's only proof that something happened at the beginning of our universe, where there wasn't space or time and then there became space and time. For many people, astronomers' discoveries confirm what they thought was true all along—that God is there. And then for many others, the discoveries of astronomers confirm what they thought all along, and that is that God is unnecessary—that God doesn't exist. The Big Bang doesn't really prove whether God (or gods) is real or not. While the universe is beautiful, complex, and fascinating, there is no evidence to show that an omniscient or divine being has to exist in order for the universe to be the way it is. But there's nothing to say that such an omniscient or divine being can't exist, either. Belief in a God (or gods) is strictly a matter of faith. Even though many theologians have expounded great thoughts on why there must be a God, such existence has not been proven or disproven by science.

One of the most famous and important theistic pragmatic arguments is *Pascal's Wager*. Blaise Pascal was born in Clermont-Ferrand, France, in 1623. His mother died when he was three years old, and he was educated by his father, Etienne, who had associations with the likes of Descartes, Mersenne, and Fermat. Blaise Pascal developed what became known as Pascal's Theorem (a work on the projective geometry of the cone) at the young age of sixteen. His other early accomplishments in mathematics included the development of probability theory and a method of infinitesimal analysis. He also made major contributions to physics, including a treatise on hydrostatics and experiments with his barometer to determine the cause of the mercury's suspension. In the area of philosophy, Pascal presented his "wager" that belief in God is a rational choice. The wager reads as follows:

> *Belief is a wise wager. Granted that faith cannot be proved, what harm will come to you if you gamble on its truth and it proves false? If you gain, you gain all; if you lose, you lose nothing. Wager, then, without hesitation, that He exists."*

In Genesis, the Bible states "*...In the beginning...God created man...in the image of God created He him.*"

**St. Basil's Cathedral on Red Square in Moscow**

Retrieved from:
http://www.moscow.info/red-square/st-basils-cathedral.aspx

Magnificent churches have been built all around the world to honor God (and gods). Some of the finest works of art adorn these churches. Liturgical music is some of the most beautiful and enduring music in existence. These works are great testimonies of faith in God (or gods). Religions provide a moral and ethical basis on which to live our lives. They provide a source of hope and consolation when we our sad or troubled, and they provide a sense of community. Religions and their rites are a means by which the social groups re-affirm themselves periodically. People feel themselves united by a community of interest and tradition, assemble and become conscious of their unity. Religion satisfies the need for emotional security. Human beings, as biological creatures, are equipped with an innate desire for self-preservation. Religion saves man from surrender to death and destruction, thus the instinct of self-preservation is at the root of belief. However, because of this instinct, we are ill-equipped to deal with our own mortality. Thus, fear of death is an important psychological determinant for the basis of the supernatural. Death remains the last bastion of faith. The psychological fear of death, stemming from the inborn instinct for self-preservation is strong. The desire to be with loved ones who have gone is also an attractive force. This explains why, even today, we become increasingly religious as we age and begin to face our own mortality.

Religion's role, as provider of the ethical, moral, and legal systems that are essential in keeping society functioning has over time been supplanted. Ethics has emerged as a social science independent of religion. In most nations, people have increasingly subscribed to a morality independent of faith—a morality which, though it may have at one point been derived by faith, no longer appeals or relies on faith to support it. The laws and tenets of religion that kept society from disintegrating have also become independent of faith. Legal systems in most nations no longer derive authority from religion, but rather from the State itself. Thus, in the collective elimination of the social and individual factors that form the very basis of faith, we can account for some decline in religion.

The primary religions of today were all founded with good intentions. Hinduism was the first to state that each person possesses a soul or spirit which can not be taken away or destroyed. Siddhartha Gautama, the Buddha, told us to "Cease to do evil; learn to do good, and purify your heart." According to tradition, God revealed his laws and commandments in the thirteenth century BC on Mount Sinai to Moses, considered Judaism's greatest prophet. The concept of an afterlife provides a reason for living a moral and just life. Jesus said, "Render unto Caesar the things which are Caesar's, and unto God the things that are God's." This phrase has become a widely quoted summary of the relationship between Christianity and secular authority. It is the reason why many countries maintain a separation of church and state.

So if religions were founded with good intentions, why has there been so much bloodshed over religions throughout the millennia? One of the basic tenets of many religions has been their propagation by various means. Religions have evolved in regions of the world to meet the social and psychological needs of the respective populations. That is well and good. However, when an attempt is made to propagate a religion into a region it is often met with existing cultural and religious differences. Religious wars are caused by, or justified by, religious differences. Such wars can involve one state with an established religion against another state with a different religion or a different sect within the same religion, or a religiously motivated group attempting to spread its faith by violence, or to suppress another group because of its religious beliefs or practices. The Muslim conquests, the French Wars of Religion, the Crusades, and the Reconquista (reconquest of the Iberian Peninsula from the Moors) are frequently cited historical examples.

Saint Augustine is credited as being the first to detail a just war theory within Christianity, whereby war is justifiable on religious grounds. Saint Thomas Aquinas elaborated on these criteria and his writings were used by the Roman Catholic Church to regulate the actions of European countries wherein Protestants and Catholics shed each others blood in prodigious amounts in national wars and civil wars during the period of the Reformation. The Muslim concept of *jihad,* which is the Arabic word for struggle, has two forms, Minor Jihad and Major Jihad. Major Jihad is the struggle to resist vice and sin and was set down in the seventh century. The concept of Minor Jihad has a combative aspect, and was set down in the tenth or eleventh century.

Many wars that are not religious wars often still include elements of religion, such as the blessing of combatants and ships headed for war. Differences in religions can further inflame a war being fought for other reasons. Historically, places of worship have been destroyed to weaken the morale of the opponent, even when the war itself is not being waged over religious ideals. Religious designations are sometimes used as shorthand for cultural and historical differences between combatants, giving the often misleading impression that a conflict is primarily about religious differences.

Religions have evolved over hundreds and even thousands of years with their belief systems deeply engrained in their members. They have evolved to meet the ethical, social, and psychological needs of populations in diverse environments. As we drift towards a more homogeneous world, religious beliefs will continue to evolve as cultures amalgamate. In a world where we can be instantaneously connected to anyone anywhere, respect for religious diversity is more essential than ever.

# Timeline for Origins of Religion

| | |
|---|---|
| Circa 4300 BC | First tombs built of huge stones appear in Western Europe. |
| 3760 BC | The first year of the Jewish calendar. |
| 3372 BC | The first year of the traditional Mayan calendar. |
| Circa 3000 BC | Scandinavian people bury their dead in passage tombs. |
| Circa 3000 BC | On Malta, people build huge megalithic temples. |
| Circa 2900 BC | According to Chinese tradition, the first divine emperors ruled. |
| Circa 2800 BC | Circular earthworks at Stonehenge in southern England become a ritual center. |
| Circa 2700 BC | Early Minoan civilization develops on Crete; religion includes worship of bulls. |
| Circa 2500 BC | Egyptians begin to mummify the corpses of the social elite. |
| Circa 2500 BC | Sumerians bury human sacrifices with their royal dead. |
| Circa 2100 BC | The first great stone circle is constructed at Stonehenge. |
| Circa 1700 BC | Ancient Greeks believe that their gods live on Mount Olympus. |
| Circa 1700 BC | In China, the kings of the Shang dynasty are buried with sacrificed servants to serve them in the afterlife. |
| Circa 1500 BC | In India, the Brahmin priesthood rises to the top of a fixed society of "castes". First Vedas are composed (hymns to the Hindu gods). |
| Circa 1500 BC | Zoroaster, a Persian aristocrat, begins to develop a new religion after visions reveal that there is one supreme god and six lesser deities. |

| | |
|---|---|
| Circa 1400 - 400 BC | Vedas, on which the Vedic religion is based, are composed over a period of 1000 years including the world's oldest sacred book, the Rig Veda upon which much of today's Hinduism is based. |
| Circa 1300 BC | According to Biblical accounts, Moses receives the Ten Commandments at Mount Sinai, Egypt. |
| Circa 1300 BC | Olmec religious rituals include cutting themselves to offer blood to their gods. |
| Circa 800 BC | The Celts of northwestern Europe hold rituals at oak trees and springs led by priests named druids; the rituals include human sacrifice. |
| Circa 800 BC | Greek athletes compete in the first Olympic games in honor of the gods of Mount Olympus. |
| Circa 600 BC | The Hebrew Bible was formed from a collection of texts around 600 BC. |
| Circa 560 BC | Birth of Siddhartha Gautama (Buddha). |
| Circa 500 BC | The Torah becomes the basis of Judaism, laying down rules for everyday life and preserving Jewish culture and ritual. |
| Circa 500 BC | In China, Confucius teaches his students his philosophy of filial devotion. |
| Circa 400 BC | Buddhism takes root and spreads through northern India. |
| 186 BC | Roman authorities suppress the hedonistic cult of Bacchus in Italy. |
| 4 BC | Probable year of the birth of Jesus. |
| 26 AD | Timeframe when Jesus of Nazareth begins preaching and attracting followers. |
| 325 AD | Emperor Constantine gives Christianity a big boost by making it the state faith throughout the Roman Empire. |
| 570 AD | Birth of the Prophet Muhammad to a merchant family in the city of Mecca. |

| | |
|---|---|
| 1100 AD | Archbishop of Canterbury, Thomas Beckett, is venerated by both Catholics and Anglicans for his martyrdom. |
| 1495 AD | Michelangelo and Leonardo da Vinci work simultaneously on *Pieta* and *The Last Supper*, respectively. |
| 1830 AD | Joseph Smith, Jr. publishes his *Book of Mormon* and starts a following called the Latter-day Saints. |
| 2005 AD | Benedict XVI elected pope when Pope John Paul II dies after being the second longest-serving pontiff at twenty-six years (Pope Pius IX served over thirty years). |

**Space Shuttle Liftoff**

Retrieved from:
http:www.nasa.gov/centers/kennedy/images/content/107053m
ain_sts-1.jpg

# CHAPTER 5

## Evolution: Science and Technology

Scientific discoveries require scientific ideas. Scientific ideas primarily act on society through technology, but they also change our sense of who we are and of what the world is. Our notions of science and scientists date only to the nineteenth century. Before then, science simply meant knowledge; the label of scientist did not exist. Instead, the study of the natural world was known as natural philosophy. The great philosophers Plato and Aristotle are today considered two of the most influential figures in the history of science.

In prehistoric times, advice and knowledge were passed from generation to generation in an oral tradition. For example, the domestication of maize for agriculture has been dated to about nine thousand years ago in southern Mexico, before the development of writing systems. Similarly, archaeological evidence indicates the development of astronomical knowledge in preliterate societies. Many ancient civilizations collected astronomical information in a systematic manner through simple observation even though they had no knowledge of the real physical structure of the planets and stars. From their beginnings in Sumer (now Iraq) around 3500 BC, the Mesopotamian people began to attempt to record some observations of the world with extremely thorough numerical data. The development of writing enabled knowledge to be stored and communicated across generations with much greater fidelity. Combined with the development of agriculture, which allowed for a surplus of food, it became possible for early civilizations to develop, because more time could be devoted to tasks other than survival.

In Babylonian astronomy, tables of the motions of the stars, planets, and the moon are left on thousands of clay tablets. Even today, astronomical periods identified by the Mesopotamians are still widely used in Western calendars such as the solar year and the lunar month. Using these data they developed arithmetical methods to compute the changing length of daylight in the course of the year and to predict the appearances and disappearances of the moon and planets and eclipses of the sun and moon.

Ancient Egypt made significant advances in astronomy, mathematics and medicine. Their development of geometry was a necessary outgrowth of surveying to preserve the layout and ownership of farmland, which was flooded annually by the Nile River. Among the Greeks, Plato and Aristotle produced the first systematic discussions of natural philosophy, which did much to shape later investigations of nature. Their development of deductive reasoning was of particular importance and usefulness to later scientific inquiry. In Greek medicine, Hippocrates (circa 460 BC – circa 370 BC) and his followers were the first to describe many diseases and medical conditions and developed the Hippocratic Oath for physicians, still relevant and in use today. The Greek mathematician Euclid laid down the foundations of mathematical rigor and introduced the concepts of definition, axiom, theorem and proof still in use today.

The willingness to question previously held truths and search for new answers resulted in a period of major scientific advancements, now known as the Scientific Revolution. The Scientific Revolution is traditionally held by most historians to have begun in 1543. It is a convenient boundary between ancient thought and classical physics. The seventeenth century "Age of Reason" opened the avenues to the decisive steps towards modern science, which took place during the eighteenth century "Age of Enlightenment." Modern science is a uniquely Western cultural phenomenon, and the combination of abstract scientific knowledge with practical know-how in the nineteenth century made possible "techno-science," which has remained a relentless driver of social change ever since. Scientists in 1900 had no inkling of the mind-boggling developments that lay in wait: plate tectonics, genetic engineering, space probes, nanotechnology, Big Bang Theory, electronic computers, nuclear weapons, artificial intelligence, and many other astounding products of the human mind.

For two hundred years now, the interaction of science and technology with society has been the primary driver of social and cultural change, first in the West, then globally at an accelerating rate. During this period, social and personal values and relationships; social, political, and economic institutions; and cultural values and activities have changed and continue to change almost beyond anything our great-grandparents (or even parents) would recognize. There are objects, of course (the telephone, automobile, airplane, television, computer, etc.) that appear to be causes of social change. But identifying these artifacts does not reach down to the causes of innovation itself, nor does it expose those features of the sociocultural infrastructure that enable innovations to become causes of social change. Artifacts, in spite of their high visibility, are symptoms of causes at work; they are not themselves causes.

The pursuit of science responds to the needs and temper of a society rather than developing according to a notion of progress. It is not only television, the automobile, or the Internet that have changed society, instead, forces at work in society have caused television and automobiles and the Internet to take on the changing forms they take. One of these forces is ideas—new scientific ideas, originating in the past and subsequently internalized by society. Many ideas languish until the right climate exists for their acceptance or rediscovery. Ideas have shaped both our social and cultural affairs and the lines along which society is most open to change. For instance, the notion that there are laws of nature seems to reflect a political idea. There can be no doubt that mathematical and aesthetic ideas were central to the seventeenth-century Scientific Revolution. Furthermore, distinguishing science from technology is often fuzzy—especially since the late nineteenth century, when scientific knowledge and technological innovation began to be coupled systematically in industrial, academic, and government research laboratories.

The idea of knowledge had to be invented. Plato and Aristotle defined knowledge as something universal, not linked to probabilities or context. For them, knowledge was timeless, universal, necessary, and certain, and their paradigm was deductive logical reasoning, as in geometry. Plato believed that true reality was form, which exists separately from matter. Aristotle broke decisively with Plato by declaring there is only one reality, which is nature, and that all natural phenomena are to be explained within the framework of nature. Parmenides posited that reality was manifested in changeless things, while Heraclitus said reality was change or process. The tension between these two approaches continues to this day. Between 500 BC and 300 BC, Greek philosophers developed highly specific concepts of knowledge, reason, truth, nature, mathematics, and logic. They used mathematics to describe nature—all in ways that continue to inform the practice of science to the present day.

Pythagoras proposed a mathematical order underlying nature and that mathematics could be used to describe natural phenomena. Although Aristotle generally dismissed the value of mathematics for the study of nature, Archimedes and others followed the example of Pythagoras. In the first century BC, the Roman architect Vitruvius wrote about the fruitful combination of abstract knowledge with practical know-how. Today we would call a person who combines both an engineer. Vitruvius did not originate this idea, but Roman society from his time forward experienced the first heyday of machines whose invention depended on mathematical knowledge.

Islamic civilization experienced a golden age under the Abbassid Dynasty, which ruled from the mid-eighth century until the mid-thirteenth century. Under the Abbassids, Islamic culture became a blending of Arab, Persian, Egyptian, and European traditions. The result was an era of stunning intellectual and cultural achievements. Islamic scholars studied both Greek and Indian mathematics before making important contributions of their own. The most well known Islamic mathematician was al-Khwarizimi, who pioneered the study of algebra. His textbook on the subject became a standard in European universities for centuries. Islamic scholars were also skilled in astronomy. They studied eclipses, the rotation of the planets, and calculated the circumference of the earth to within a few thousand feet. Many advances were also made in the field of medicine. Physicians and pharmacists were required to pass exams before treating patients. They setup hospitals that had separate areas for trauma cases; this is the basis for today's emergency rooms. Physicians developed treatments for cataracts, used a variety of herbal remedies, and were adept at treating a variety of injuries.

Islamic pharmacists were the first to mix sweet-tasting syrups with medicine, ensuring that they would be taken. Ibn Sina, a famous Islamic physician, wrote a book called *Canon on Medicine*, which was an encyclopedia of Greek, Arabic, and his own knowledge of medicine. This book became the standard medical text in Europe for over five hundred years.

As Europe was absorbing the fruits of Islam's centuries of creative productivity, signs of Latin Christian awakening were evident throughout the European continent. The twelfth century was one of intensified traffic of Muslim learning into the Western world through many hundreds of translations of Muslim works, which helped Europe seize the initiative from Islam when political conditions in Islam brought about a decline in Muslim scholarship. Social pressure to make life better and to explore knowledge spawned universities across Europe. By 1300, European scholars stood once again on the solid ground of Hellenistic thought, enriched or modified through Muslim and Byzantine efforts.

From the twelfth through the sixteenth centuries, universities revived and extended Classical and Islamic learning in mathematics, philosophy, medicine, and science. Parallel with the rise of universities was an explosion of technical skills supporting the development of water mills, sawmills, blast furnaces, and the like. The most famous gear-related invention of the age was the weight-driven mechanical clock. Improved sailing and navigation technologies supported increased trade. Banks and corporations were established.

The notion of progress did not begin with technology but with Petrarch and a concern about language. Humanist scholars developed scholarly techniques for reconstructing Classical texts then sought to surpass Classical learning. The Humanist idea of progress paved the way for the idea of social reform based on scientific reason. Printing of texts and movable type were old technologies when Gutenberg introduced the latter to Europe. Unlike China and the Middle East, the West embraced metallic movable type and became print drunk. The response triggered the creation of a vast sociotechnic system to supply, produce, and distribute texts. Institutions were created to protect and reward producers and increase literacy, promoting further increases in text production and distribution.

The technique of perspective used by Renaissance painters made visual the notion that reality is structured by mathematics. The rebirth of techno-science depended largely on their work, with further contributions by Renaissance mapmaking, instrument tuning (musical theory), and books illustrating the design of machines.

Pythagoreans claimed that astronomical bodies were spheres, their orbits circles, and their motion constant because they were perfect. Copernicus replaced Ptolemy's Earth-centered model with a sun-centered model, but it remained for his followers to make the planetary orbits elliptical, rather than circular, and posit an infinite universe. Bringing together all of the ideas discussed to this point was the seventeenth century's idea of modern science. A new emphasis on scientific method was a critical factor in pulling everything together, though founding figures of this period such as René Descartes and Francis Bacon championed radically different methods.

During the sixteenth and seventeenth centuries, mathematics in the West took a remarkable turn. It moved from geometry, which the ancient Greeks had favored, to algebra — which was as momentous as the transition from Ptolemaic astronomy to Copernican astronomy. Calculus provided an unprecedented tool for knowledge about change, and the mathematics of probability opened the way for knowledge about uncertainty. Experience suggests that nature is orderly and lawful; if so, then something has to be conserved. From this notion slowly developed the ideas of conservation of momentum, matter, and energy; Einstein's idea that matter and energy are jointly conserved; and the use of mathematical invariances to understand deep symmetries in nature. Galileo saw what he described as moons around Jupiter in the seventeenth century, but his description could not be verified independently for many years. If a scientific instrument gives a result that cannot be verified independently, then the result is really an extension of the mind rather than of the senses. This is no less true today. Particle accelerators, for example, provide mountains of mathematical data that require interpretation.

An idea becomes a scientific idea when it functions in the context of a scientific explanation. The idea of time is an excellent example. If, as Plato claimed, both real knowledge and ultimate reality are timeless, then time is insignificant. However, by the eighteenth century, the idea of time was increasingly regarded as the dimension containing hope for an improvement in the human condition. This, in turn, prefigured nineteenth-century scientific ideas of time as both irreversible and significant. The theory of the atom began as an extension of Parmenides' view of reality as ultimately changeless. John Dalton in the early nineteenth century used a theory of changeless atoms in his examination of chemical reactions, and atomism gained prominence thereafter even as the atom was discovered to be mainly empty space and composed of parts, each with distinct properties.

What is life? An eighteenth-century debate pitting mechanism against vitalism was resolved, literally, when new microscopes of the early nineteenth century were used to proclaim in the late 1830s that cells were the building blocks of all living things. The view that cells were the atoms of life, in turn, provoked a search for what within the cell is the essence of life. The germ theory of disease is another instance of the atomistic style of thinking and the cornerstone of modern scientific medicine. The notion of disease caused by imbalances within the body was undermined when Pasteur and Koch showed how illness comes from the outside, an idea dating back to Hippocrates and the notion of miasmas. Resistance to the germ theory was understandable; some people had germs in their bodies but not the disease. Gregor Mendel was trying to confirm a theory about evolution when his experiments with pea plants led him to realize that inheritance was owed to discrete units. Mendel demonstrated that the inheritance of certain traits in pea plants followed particular patterns, now referred to as the laws of Mendelian inheritance. Although the significance of Mendel's work was not recognized until the turn of the twentieth century, the independent rediscovery of these laws formed the foundation of the modern science of genetics. Yet gene theory rests less on Mendel's work than on later experiments with fruit flies showing that X-rays could alter parts of chromosomes. If X-rays could do that, then genes must be real.

In the nineteenth century, with the rise of the science of thermodynamics, energy assumed a parallel reality to matter. Like matter, energy was seen to take many forms but was conserved. Unlike matter, the idea of energy quickly stimulated process theories in which patterns and relationships were real. Faraday's introduction of fields as elements of physical reality in the nineteenth century was a giant step for modern science, but the difficulty of formulating a plausible physical mechanism for how fields work led to Maxwell's equations of electrodynamics—and a view of scientific theories as capturing our experience of a process, rather than a final truth about objects.

Beginning in 1837, a few chemists came to believe that understanding a molecule required knowing not only what atoms the molecule had, but also the spatial relationships among those atoms. This insight forms one of the cornerstones of organic chemistry. Pasteur relied on this insight. The recognition of relationships as real also appeared in other nineteenth-century disciplines including symbolic logic, mathematics, and social science.

Evolution has proven to be a cross-disciplinary idea, bringing contingency into scientific explanation and showing how novelty can emerge. Evolution also entails making time, which moves in one direction only, a fundamental feature of reality. Modern science was founded on determinism, but determinism was undermined by the recognition of probability in nature and by the claim that certain processes obeyed statistical laws. The kinetic theory of gases, thermodynamics, and radioactivity all showed that statistical laws had a place in scientific theory. This had far-reaching implications in that if nature is probabilistic, then so also are theories and laws of nature.

A qualitative divide separates important eighteenth-century innovations in textiles, iron, and steam power from such nineteenth- and twentieth-century innovations as electric power, plastics, and radio—the latter were made possible by science-informed engineering. Successful innovations became increasingly dependent on scientific knowledge and formally trained engineering, as well as supportive business acumen. Moving beyond improved versions of what already existed, such as water power, innovations increasingly appeared that could never have existed without scientific knowledge. Western societies accelerated this development by creating institutions explicitly designed to promote science-based innovation, including widespread engineering education, new ways of organizing companies, and supportive government policies.

Quantum physics is the most revolutionary of twentieth-century theories, and it is the most predictively successful physical theory ever. But it is still controversial as well as inconsistent with the general theory of relativity. Quantum mechanics imputes randomness, probability, and uncertainty to elementary physical processes. It redefines causality, space, time, matter, energy, the nature of scientific law and explanation, and the relationship between mind and world. Einstein's special theory of relativity forced a reconceptualization of Newtonian space and time and proclaimed that matter and energy could be converted into one another. The general theory even redefined physical reality at the cosmological level. The properties of space and time are determined by the distribution of matter and energy; space and time are really names of relationships, not separate in their own right. Quantum physics is leading us to look deeper into Einstein's theory of relativity and into elementary physical processes.

In the 1920s, the scale of the universe changed dramatically with the discovery of thousands of galaxies beyond our Milky Way and the expansion of the universe. By 1963, the expanding universe was explained with a "Big Bang," and by 1980, an explanation of the big bang led to the proposal that the universe was unimaginably more vast than anything we could detect.

Alan Turing conceived of a machine that could solve any problem whose solution could be specified by a finite decision procedure, or algorithm. Turing recognized that increasingly powerful calculators could be reconceived as generalized problem-solving machines, even artificially intelligent machines. Turing is widely considered to be the father of computer science and artificial intelligence. The computer went from being a calculator to a universal simulator. The evolution of the Internet from a modest U.S. Department of Defense-funded computer network project (ARPANET) to a global technology has transformed commerce, industry, politics, warfare, communication, education, entertainment, and research. We are still unfolding the unexpected and sometimes disturbing consequences of a few innovative ideas that enable computers in different locations to share information in real time—ideas that underlie the Internet's astonishing capabilities. And now, social networking is having a remarkable effect on the way people share information.

Atomistic thinking faces challenges from three closely related ideas from the twentieth century: Phenomena are produced by systems; chaotic real-world systems are in fact orderly; and some systems are self-organizing. These systems display properties that aren't apparent in the properties of their individual constituents. That is, the wholes are more than the sums of their parts.

The molecular theory of life says that life can be fully explained in terms of molecules in action, using the concepts and the tools of physics and chemistry. The discovery that DNA molecules defined every life form on Earth sealed this shift. By the 1980s, the molecular theory of life was transforming medicine as well as the meaning of life. Genetic therapies and biomedical enhancements are becoming a multibillion-dollar industry. New techniques will enable doctors to change your DNA to revitalize old or diseased organs, enhance your appearance, increase your athletic ability, or boost your intelligence.

Which scientific ideas will transform twenty-first-century life? Self-organization is fundamental to the emerging nanotechnology industry. Molecular biology and cognitive neuroscience continue their naturalization of human consciousness. Quantum chemistry makes possible molecular psychiatry and even molecular sociology. String theory controversially promises to unify the forces of nature into a comprehensive theory of everything.

A new revolution in computing may make computers exponentially faster than today based on the strange behavior of matter at the quantum level. The basic unit of a quantum computer is a "qubit"—an electron spinning either clockwise or counter clockwise, representing a 0 or a 1. Because electrons can coexist in two places simultaneously, a single electron can carry two qubits, two electrons can produce four qubits, three electrons, eight, and twenty electrons could perform a million computations. The exponential growth raises the hope of infinite processing power. A quantum computer could easily complete in seconds a task that would take a silicon computer billions of years. The first research prototypes are now running at Harvard University, the National Security Agency, and the Federal Reserve. These revolutionary computers may be on the market by 2020.

Water desalination may soon become one of the world's largest industries. By 2040, at least 3.5 billion people will run short of water—almost ten times as many as in 1995. The huge demand, plus new more efficient desalination technologies, will create enormous profit opportunities and bring new life to arid regions. A Canadian company, Element Four, has developed a machine that it hopes will become the first mainstream household appliance to have been invented since the microwave. Their creation, the WaterMill, uses the electricity of about three light bulbs to condense moisture from the air and purify it into clean drinking water. By the year 2020 these could well be in common use and provide a needed source of clean water in places where it is desperately needed.

"A Timeline of Science and Technology" is provided at the end of this chapter. While only some highlights are listed, it is obvious that science and technology are evolving at an accelerating rate. The human population is growing at an accelerating rate (reference "Growth of Human Population" chart in Chapter 2). The availability of information is expanding exponentially with the advent of computers and the Internet. Because of the explosive nature of exponential growth, the twenty-first century could well be equivalent to twenty thousand years of progress at today's rate of progress; about one thousand times greater than the twentieth century. We are infants in the realm of science and technology. We have barely scratched the surface of what there is to know. There is infinitely more to learn and accomplish as we evolve.

On the negative side, in the twenty-first century we will see disasters occur with surprising frequency. There are several reasons for this. We have chosen to engineer the planet. We have built vast networks of technology. We have created systems such as nuclear power plants that, in general, work very well, but are still vulnerable to catastrophic failures. It is harder and harder for any one person, institution, or agency to perceive all the interconnected elements of the technological society. Failures can cascade. There are unseen weak points in the network. Small failures can have broad consequences. Most importantly, we have more people and more things being affected by calamities. We are not suddenly having more earthquakes, but there are now 7 billion of us, a majority living in cities. In 1800, only Beijing could count a million inhabitants, but at last count there were 381 cities with at least 1 million people. Many are "megacities" in seismically hazardous places—Mexico City, Caracas, Tehran, and Kathmandu being among those with a lethal combination of weak infrastructure and unreinforced masonry buildings. Natural disasters will increasingly be accompanied by technological crises, and the other way around. The Japan earthquake in 2011 triggered the Fukushima Daiichi nuclear power plant meltdown. A technological failure coupled with insufficient human oversight in 2011 on the Deepwater Horizon drilling rig in the Gulf of Mexico led to the environmental crisis of the oil spill.

## Some Predictions

Current methods of high speed scanning make it possible to get a 3D scan of your face in a fraction of a second. 3D televisions are already available in the marketplace. Tomorrow's 3D televisions won't require special glasses or even screens. A company in Burlington, Massachusetts, the Z Corporation, has developed a 3D printer that can actually produce 3D objects. Using a hand-held scanner, one can scan an object such as a tool and a copy can be made out of a proprietary composite material. Mathematicians in Finland have produced a blueprint for instruments that will project floating 3D images by means of nanomaterials that bend light around objects. In the near future, projecting an image of yourself or a room full a people to another location as a hologram will be commonplace.

Often described as "Wi-Fi on steroids," WiMAX (Worldwide Interoperability for Microwave Access) will cover entire countries with a vibrant, high-speed wireless communications network. Internet access and other data and video applications will be available anywhere including many applications for automobiles.

By 2025, the worldwide average life-span will be extended every two years by one year—only 15% of deaths worldwide will be due to naturally occurring infectious diseases. On the negative side, bioviolence will become a greater threat. In the next decade, biological technologies that were once at the frontiers of science will become available to anyone with minimal scientific training. Emerging biotechnologies, such as genomics and nanotechnology, will make it possible for those with bad intentions to alter bacteria and viruses to increase their lethality or make them more resistant to antibiotics.

By 2050, the United States will get most of its energy from sources other than oil. Fusion power will be available. Fusion power has almost no nuclear waste. We will have computers that will be able to simulate the human brain and will be able to converse like people with people. Computers will have the capacity to store all of the information contained in the human brain. For those that can afford immortality, their brains could be scanned and downloaded to machines, perhaps to be uploaded to a new brain. Cancer and AIDS will be cured. By 2050,

Alzheimer's disease will be treatable such that its progression can be halted and reversed. Artificial limbs will outperform natural ones. Astronauts will land on Mars, and ordinary people will travel in space. Extinct species will be able to be resuscitated through cloning. Evidence of life will be found elsewhere in our universe. The number of electric-powered cars will greatly exceed the number of gas-powered cars.

New satellites, high tech measuring equipment and more powerful supercomputers are helping scientists and researchers learn more about the weather patterns of the earth. By 2050 you can expect more accurate weather predictions and eventually, controlling the weather itself. Governments throughout the world are researching weather modification. Potential benefits of controlling the weather would be increased crop yields, decreasing the severity of storms, accurate forecasts, eliminating drought, stopping global warming, protection from harmful solar energy, and clear skies for astronomers, air traffic, and solar panels. There are also military uses, such as making sure the weather is clear for a mission or covering the enemy with snow, fog, hail or lightning strikes. A far better use of weather modification would be if we could someday stop a hurricane like Katrina from ever reaching land. That would be a future to behold.

Brain machine interfaces (BMIs) are currently in their infancy. They allow for activity in the brain to be sent to, or received from, a computer. Some BMIs use sensors mounted in a removable cap. Others use MRI technology to read signals from the brain. Still others connect directly to the surface of the brain, through tiny wires and an array of nano-electrodes. BMIs can also be entirely implanted in the brain. Brain machine interfaces are currently assisting paralyzed patients communicate, control robotic arms, computers, and other devices. In the future, BMIs could provide a path to brain enhancement and memory upload/download.

By 2100, we could well be able to manipulate objects with the power of our minds. Computers, silently reading our thoughts, might be able to carry out our wishes. We might be able to move objects by thought alone. With the power of biotechnology, we will create more perfect bodies and extend our life spans. We will also be able to create life—forms that have never walked the surface of the earth. With the power of nanotechnology, we will be able to take an object and turn it into something else, to create something seemingly almost out of nothing. We will ride in sleek vehicles that will soar by themselves with almost no fuel, floating effortlessly in the air. With our engines, we will be able to harness the limitless energy of the stars. We will also be on the threshold of sending star ships to explore nearby stars and planets. Our tools will be the science of computers, nanotechnology, artificial intelligence, biotechnology, and most of all, quantum theory, which is the foundation of many technologies.

Mankind may one day create a machine that could quite possibly threaten our very existence. One cannot rule out the point in time when machine intelligence will eventually surpass human intelligence. These super intelligent machine creations could possibly become self-aware, have their own agenda and may even one day be able to create copies of themselves that are more intelligent than they are.

Today we are striving towards a global economy. We can communicate with anyone on our planet. Commerce, trade, culture, language, entertainment, and leisure activities are all being revolutionized by the emergence of a global civilization. All of the civilizations from the past are evolving towards this modern day civilization. With the world's rapidly expanding population, it will be necessary to work as a united civilization to meet growing needs. In so doing, we will become a more homogenous people and sadly there will be much less in the way of cultural and ethnic differences. By 2100, one can predict that we will have made the transition to a global civilization. In the words of Martin Luther King, Jr.: "We must learn to live together as brothers or perish together as fools."

# Timeline of Science and Technology

## BC

24th century BC
- The abacus, the first known calculator, invented in Babylonia.

17th century BC
- Venus tablet of Ammisaduqa: first known Babylonian astronomical observations.

8th century BC
- *Aitareya Brahmana* (an ancient Indian collection of sacred hymns written in Sanskrit): heliocentrism – sun-centered universe.

6th century BC
- Babylonian base-60 math system, still in use today for telling time (60 minutes in an hour), measuring angles, and performing astronomical computations (60 minutes in a degree).

430s BC
- Democritus: Accurate atomic hypothesis.

360s BC
- Eudoxus of Cnidus: Greek mathematician and astronomer who mapped the stars and compiled a map of the known world.

350s BC
- Heraclides: Greek astronomer who proposed that the earth rotates on its axis once a day.

300 BC
- Pingala: author of the Chandaḥúâstra (also Chandaḥsûtra) which presents the first known description of a binary numeral system in Sanskrit.

3rd century BC
- Eratosthenes: calculated the size of the earth and its distance to the sun and to the moon.
- Archimedes: mathematically worked out the principle of the lever and discovers the principle of buoyancy.

150s BC
- Seleucus of Seleucia: discovery of tides being caused by the moon.

87 BC
- Antikythera Mechanism invented in Rhodes to track movement of the stars.

## AD

150s
- Ptolemy: produced the geocentric model of the solar system.

724
- Liang Ling-Can: Invents the first fully mechanical clock.

8th century
- Beginning of chemistry and experimental method; discovery of hydrochloric, sulfuric, nitric and acetic acids; discovery of soda, potash and pure alcohol (ethanol); the discovery that aqua regia, a mixture of nitric and hydrochloric acids, could dissolve metals such as gold; and discovery of liquefaction, purification by crystallization, purification, oxidation, evaporation, filtration and sublimation.

9th century
- Ja'far Muhammad ibn Mûsâ ibn Shâkir: discovery of the heavenly bodies and celestial spheres being subject to the same physical laws as the earth; and the existence of gravitation between heavenly bodies and within the celestial

spheres (precursor to Newton's law of universal gravitation).

- Al-Kindi (Alkindus): the concept of relativity; and refutation of the theory of the transmutation of metals.

10th century
- Muhammad ibn Zakarîya Râzi (Rhazes): discovery of measles and smallpox.

11th century
- 1021 – Ibn al-Haytham's : beginning of modern optics, scientific method and experimental physics; correct explanation of visual perception; invention of camera obscura and pinhole camera; foundations of telescopic astronomy; discovery of light rays traveling in straight lines and being made up of energy particles, Fermat's principle of least time, and vision being caused by light rays entering the eye; the rectilinear propagation, constituent colors and electromagnetic aspects of light; explanations of shadows, binocular vision, atmospheric refraction and the moon illusion; the relationship of the density of the atmosphere with altitude; and the finite speed of light.
- 1020s – Avicenna's *The Canon of Medicine*: beginning of experimental medicine; discovery of the contagious nature of infectious diseases, including phthisis, tuberculosis and sexually transmitted disease; and the discovery of mediastinitis and pleurisy, bacteria and viral organisms, and the distribution of disease through water and soil.
- Ibn al-Haytham and Avicenna: law of inertia (Newton's first law of motion) and discovery of momentum (part of Newton's second law of motion).
- Ibn al-Haytham: attraction between masses and the magnitude of acceleration due to gravity at a distance.
- Abû Rayhân al-Bîrûnî: beginning of experimental astronomy and experimental mechanics; discovery of the Milky Way galaxy being a collection of numerous nebulous stars; and the discovery that the solar apogee and the precession are not identical; the finite speed of light being

much faster than the speed of sound; and the relationship between acceleration and non-uniform motion (part of Newton's second law of motion).
- 1041 – Bi Sheng: invented movable type printing press.

12th century
- 1121 – Al-Khazini: variation of gravitation and gravitational potential energy at a distance; the decrease of air density with altitude.
- Ibn Bajjah (Latinized name is Avempace): discovery of reaction (precursor to Newton's third law of motion).
- Hibat Allah Abu'l-Barakat al-Baghdaadi (Latinized name is Nathanel): relationship between force and acceleration (a vague foreshadowing of a fundamental law of classical mechanics and a precursor to Newton's second law of motion).
- Averroes: relationship between force, work, and kinetic energy.

13th century
- 1220–1235 – Robert Grosseteste: rudiments of the scientific method.
- 1242 – Ibn al-Nafis: pulmonary circulation and circulatory system.
- 1280 – Eyeglasses were invented.

14th century
- Pre 1327 – William of Ockham: Occam's Razor - cut out all features of a theory that cannot be observed.

15th century
- 1450 – Johann Gutenberg: alphabetic, movable type printing press.
- 1490 – Leonardo da Vinci: describes capillary action.
- 1500 –Leonardo da Vinci: invents ball bearings, the first mechanical calculator, one of the first programmable robots, and proposes flying machines including a helicopter.

16th century
- 1510 – Peter Henlien: Pocket watch.
- 1543 – Copernicus: heliocentric model – sun centered universe.
- 1543 – Vesalius: pioneering research into human anatomy.
- 1552 – Michael Servetus: early research in Europe into pulmonary circulation.
- 1570s – Tycho Brahe: detailed astronomical observations.
- 1581 – Galileo Galilei: notices the timekeeping property of the pendulum.
- 1589 – Galileo Galilei: uses balls rolling on inclined planes to show that different weights fall with the same acceleration.
- 1593 – Galileo Galilei: invents thermometer.
- 1600 – William Gilbert: Earth's magnetic field.

17th century
- 1604 – Johannes Kepler: describes how the eye focuses light.
- 1608 – Hans Lippershey: invents telescope.
- 1609 – Johannes Kepler: first two laws of planetary motion.
- 1609 – Galileo Galilei: invents microscope.
- 1609 – Galileo Galilei: builds his first optical refracting telescope.
- 1610 – Galileo Galilei: *Sidereus Nuncius*: telescopic observations.
- 1614 – John Napier: use of logarithms for calculation.
- 1628 – William Harvey: first person to describe completely and in detail the systemic blood circulation.
- 1642 – Blaise Pascal: invents adding machine.
- 1643 – Evangelista Torricelli: invents the mercury barometer.
- 1645 – Otto von Guericke: invents vacuum pump.
- 1657 – Christiaan Huygens: invents pendulum clock.
- 1662 – Robert Boyle: Boyle's law of ideal gas.

- 1665 – Philosophical Transactions of the Royal Society first peer reviewed scientific journal published.
- 1668 – John Wallis: suggests the law of conservation of momentum.
- 1668 – Isaac Newton: constructs the first optical reflecting telescope.
- 1669 – Nicholas Steno: Proposes that fossils are organic remains embedded in layers of sediment, basis of stratigraphy.
- 1669 – Jan Swammerdam: Species breed true.
- 1675 – Leibniz, Newton: Infinitesimal calculus.
- 1675 – Anton van Leeuwenhoek: Observes Microorganisms by Microscope.
- 1676 – Ole Rømer: first measurement of the speed of light.
- 1687 – Newton: Laws of motion, law of universal gravitation, basis for classical physics.
- 1698 – Thomas Savery invents steam engine.

18th century
- 1705 – Thomas Newcomen invents steam piston engine.
- 1708 – Jethro Tull invents mechanical seed sower.
- 1728 – James Bradley discovers the aberration of starlight and uses it to determine that the speed of light is about 283,000 km/s.
- 1745 – Ewald Jürgen Georg von Kleist develops first capacitor, the Leyden jar.
- 1750 – Joseph Black describes latent heat.
- 1751 – Benjamin Franklin: Lightning is electrical.
- 1766 – Henry Cavendish discovers and studies hydrogen.
- 1769 – James Watt reinvents the steam engine.
- 1771 – Joseph Priestly discovers that plants convert carbon dioxide into oxygen.
- 1778 – Antoine Lavoisier (and Joseph Priestley): discovery of oxygen leading to end of Phlogiston theory.
- 1779 – First steam powered mills automate weaving process.

- 1781 – William Herschel announces discovery of Uranus, expanding the known boundaries of the solar system for the first time in modern history.
- 1783 – Montgolfier brothers invent hot air balloon.
- 1785 – William Withering publishes the first definitive account of the use of foxglove (digitalis) for treating dropsy.
- 1787 – Jacques Charles: Charles' law of ideal gas.
- 1789 – Antoine Lavoisier: law of conservation of mass, basis for chemistry, and the beginning of modern chemistry.
- 1791 – John Fitch invents steamboat.
- 1793 – Eli Whitney develops the cotton gin.
- 1796 – Georges Cuvier: Establishes extinction as a fact.
- 1798 – Edward Jenner invents vaccinations.
- 1799 – William Smith: Publishes geologic map of England, first geologic map ever, first application of stratigraphy.
- 1800 – William Herschel discovers infrared radiation from the sun.

19th century
- 1801 – Johann Ritter: discovers ultraviolet radiation from the sun.
- 1802 – Jean-Baptiste Lamarck: teleological (purposeful) evolution.
- 1804 – Richard Trevithick invents locomotive.
- 1805 – John Dalton: Atomic Theory in (Chemistry).
- 1820 – Hans Oersted: notices that a current in a wire can deflect a compass needle.
- 1821 – Michael Faraday invents electric motor.
- 1822 – Charles Babbage designs the first mechanical computer.
- 1824 – Carnot described the Carnot cycle, the idealized heat engine.
- 1826 – Joseph Nicephore Niepce invents photography.
- 1827 – Georg Ohm: Ohm's law (Electricity).
- 1827 – Amedeo Avogadro: Avogadro's law (Gas laws).

- 1828 – Friedrich Wöhler: synthesized urea, destroying vitalism.
- 1831 – Michael Faraday discovers electro-magnetic current, making possible generators and electric motors.
- 1833 – Anselme Payen isolates first enzyme, diastase.
- 1838 – Matthias Schleiden declares all plants are made of cells.
- 1838 – Charles Wheatstone and Samual Morse invent electric telegraph.
- 1839 – Charles Goodyear invents vulcanization of rubber.
- 1842 – Christian Doppler examines the Doppler shift of sound.
- 1842 – Crawford Long invents anesthesia.
- 1843 – James Prescott Joule: Law of Conservation of energy (First law of thermodynamics), also 1847 – Helmholtz, Conservation of energy.
- 1845 – Michael Faraday discovers light propagation in a material can be influenced by external magnetic fields.
- 1846 – Elias Howe invents sewing machine.
- 1847 – Hermann Helmholtz:formally states the law of conservation of energy.
- 1848 – Lord Kelvin: absolute zero of temperature.
- 1849 – Armand Fizeau and Jean-Bernard Foucault measure the speed of light to be about 298,000 km/s.
- 1851 – Jean-Bernard Foucault shows the Earth's rotation with a huge pendulum.
- 1858 – Rudolf Virchow: cells can only arise from pre-existing cells.
- 1859 – Charles Darwin and Alfred Wallace: Theory of evolution by natural selection.
- 1864 – James Clerk Maxwell publishes his papers on a dynamical theory of the electromagnetic field.
- 1865 – Gregor Mendel: Mendel's laws of inheritance, basis for genetics.
- 1869 – Dmitri Mendeleev: Periodic table (Chemistry).
- 1873 – James Clerk Maxwell: Theory of electromagnetism; states that light is an electromagnetic phenomenon.

- 1873 – Johannes van der Waals: introduces the idea of weak attractive forces between molecules.
- 1875 – William Crookes inventes the Crookes tube and studies cathode rays.
- 1876 – Josiah Willard Gibbs founds chemical thermodynamics, the phase rule.
- 1877 – Ludwig Boltzmann: Statistical definition of entropy.
- 1877 – Thomas Edison invents phonograph.
- 1879 – Thomas Edison patents the carbon-thread incandescent lamp.
- 1885 – Benz develops first automobile to run on internal combustion engine.
- 1888 – Heinrich Hertz discovers radio waves.
- 1893 – Nikola Tesla invents wireless communication.
- 1895 – Wilhelm Conrad Röntgen discovers x-rays.
- 1896 – Henri Becquerel discovers radioactivity.
- 1897 – J.J. Thomson discovers the electron in cathode rays.
- 1898 – Marie Curie and Pierre Curie isolate and study radium and polonium.
- 1900 – Max Planck: Planck's law of black body radiation, basis for quantum theory.

20th century
- 1903 – Wright brothers invent powered airplane.
- 1905 – Albert Einstein: theory of special relativity; explanation of Brownian motion, and photoelectric effect; states the law of mass-energy conservation.
- 1906 – Walther Nernst: Third law of thermodynamics.
- 1906 – Charles Barkla discovers that each chemical element has a characteristic X-ray and that the degree of penetration of these X-rays is related to the atomic weight of the element.
- 1907 – Auguste and Louis Lumiere invent color photography.
- 1908 – Hans Geiger and Ernest Rutherford invent the Geiger counter.

- 1909 – Fritz Haber: Haber Process.
- 1912 – Alfred Wegener: Continental drift.
- 1912 – Max von Laue : x-ray diffraction.
- 1913 – Henry Moseley defines atomic number.
- 1913 – Niels Bohr: Model of the atom.
- 1914 – Ernest Rutherford suggests that the positively charged atomic nucleus contains protons.
- 1915 – Albert Einstein: theory of general relativity – also David Hilbert.
- 1915 – Karl Schwarzschild: discovery of the Schwarzschild radius leading to the identification of black holes.
- 1918 – Emmy Noether: Noether's theorem – conditions under which the conservation laws are valid.
- 1924 – Wolfgang Pauli: quantum Pauli Exclusion Principle.
- 1924 – Edwin Hubble: the discovery that the Milky Way is just one of many galaxies.
- 1925 – Erwin Schrödinger: Schrödinger equation (Quantum mechanics).
- 1927 – Werner Heisenberg: Uncertainty principle (Quantum mechanics).
- 1927 – Georges Lemaître: Theory of the Big Bang.
- 1928 – Paul Dirac: Dirac equation (Quantum mechanics).
- 1928 – Alexander Fleming invents penicillin.
- 1929 – Edwin Hubble: Hubble's law of the expanding universe.
- 1929 – Lars Onsager: reciprocal relations, a potential fourth law of thermodynamics.
- 1934 – Clive McCay: Calorie Restriction extends the maximum lifespan of a species.
- 1934 – Leo Szilard realizes that nuclear chain reactions may be possible.
- 1934 – Ernest Lawrence and Stan Livingston invent the cyclotron.
- 1942 – Enrico Fermi makes the first controlled nuclear chain reaction.

- 1943 – Oswald Avery proves that DNA is the genetic material of the chromosome.
- 1945 – First nuclear fission bomb exploded at a test site.
- 1947 – William Shockley, John Bardeen and Walter Brattain invent the first transistor.
- 1948 – Claude Elwood Shannon: *A mathematical theory of communication*, a seminal paper in Information theory.
- 1948 – Richard Feynman, Julian Schwinger, Sin-Itiro Tomonaga and Freeman Dyson: Quantum electrodynamics.
- 1948 – George Gamow, Ralph Alpher, and Robert Herman: predict that a Big Bang universe will have a blackbody cosmic microwave background with temperature about 5° K (more recent estimates are about 2.725 ° K).
- 1951 – George Otto Gey propagates first cancer cell line, HeLa.
- 1952 – First thermonuclear fusion bomb exploded.
- 1953 – Crick and Watson: helical structure of DNA, basis for molecular biology.
- 1954 – Construction of the first nuclear power reactor.
- 1960 – Theodore Maiman makes the first laser.
- 1961 – Uri Gagarin: first man in space.
- 1964 – Murray Gell-Mann and George Zweig postulate quarks leading to the standard model.
- 1964 – Arno Penzias and Robert Woodrow Wilson: detection of Cosmic Microwave Background providing experimental evidence for the Big Bang.
- 1965 – Leonard Hayflick: normal cells divide only a certain number of times: the Hayflick limit.
- 1967 – Jocelyn Bell Burnell and Antony Hewish discover first pulsar.
- 1969 – Neil Armstrong: first person to set foot on the moon.
- 1980 – Alan Guth proposes the inflationary Big Bang universe.
- 1984 – Kary Mullis invents the polymerase chain reaction, a key discovery in molecular biology.

- Tom Berners-Lee invents World Wide Web.
- 1995 – Michel Mayor and Didier Queloz definitively observe the first extrasolar planet around a main sequence star.
- 1997 – Roslin Institute: Dolly the sheep was cloned.
- 1997 – CDF and DØ experiments at Fermilab: Top quark mass and width measurements.
- 1998 – Gerson Goldhaber and Saul Perlmutter observe that the expansion of the universe is accelerating.

21st century
- 2003 – The human genome project to discover all the estimated 20,000-25,000 human genes and make them accessible for further biological study is completed. Also the complete sequencing of the 3 billion DNA subunits is completed.
- 2006 – Pluto is formally re-classified as a dwarf planet by the International Astronomical Union.
- 2010 – J. Craig Venter Institute creates the first synthetic bacterial cell.

# CHAPTER 6

## Evolution: The Big Picture

Everything evolves over time and usually for the better. It is a reason to have hope and look for better tomorrows. While there are many evolutionary processes which we currently have no control of, there are others that over time we have come to understand and have learned to manipulate and use to our advantage. As our science and technology evolves we will have more control over natural processes. One thing we can be certain of is change.

Understanding of our universe has evolved from being Earth centered, to being sun centered with Earth being one of nine planets orbiting it, to being part of the Milky Way galaxy with hundreds of billions of stars of which our sun is just one. And, from the Hubble telescope, we now know that Earth is just one of eight planets in orbit around the Sun (Pluto being downgraded to a dwarf planet in August 2006) in a galaxy containing hundreds of billions of stars, in a universe containing hundreds of billions of galaxies. Now we are learning that perhaps our universe is one of many in a cosmos of universes sometimes referred to as a multiverse. We have just scratched the surface of what there is to learn about the cosmos.

The past of human evolution is increasingly coming to light as scientists uncover a trove of fossils and genetic knowledge. But where might the future of human evolution go? We know that we are still evolving to adapt to different and changing environments. Now humanity has an unparalleled means by which to direct our evolution—genetic engineering. By using viruses and other techniques, we can in theory modify our genomes, and over time, scientists may uncover genes underlying intelligence, health, athletic prowess, longevity and other desirable traits, engineering what might seem like superhuman progeny. The ethical and religious outlook on genetic engineering in humans remains to be sorted out.

Humans have evolved from communicating orally with their hunter-gatherer neighbors, to pictorially on cave walls and clay tablets, to written language on scrolls, to printed books available to the masses; and now, electronically, much of the world's accumulated knowledge is available to anyone, anywhere, at anytime via the Internet. The ability to store this knowledge on electronic media and make it available to everyone is rapidly propelling advancements in all facets of life, science, and technology. The Internet is having a profound effect on how people acquire knowledge and how they communicate. It has been said that mankind has made more progress in the twentieth century than in all of previous history, and that the twenty-first century could well be equivalent to twenty thousand years of progress at today's rate of progress; about one thousand times greater than the twentieth century.

Today humanity is striving toward a global economy. We can communicate with anyone anywhere on our planet. Commerce, trade, culture, language, entertainment, and leisure activities are all being revolutionized by the emergence of a global civilization. All of the civilizations from the past are evolving towards this modern day civilization. With the world's rapidly expanding population, it will be necessary to work in a united way to meet growing needs. In so doing, we will become a more homogenous people, but sadly there will be much less in the way of cultural and ethnic differences. By 2100, one can predict that we will have made the transition to a global civilization.

Global politics will become more important in the future. There will be increasing interdependencies between countries in a global civilization. Still, the needs of a growing global population will exert stresses on countries which could put the whole world on a wartime footing. While science and technology will continue to contribute to meeting the needs of the world, political leadership will become more important than ever in administering to those needs.

As cultures have evolved, religions have evolved to meet the ethical, social, spiritual, and psychological needs of diverse populations. Many religious beliefs are based on faith and not science. As science explains more about our universe and life, there is less for religion to explain. Our universe is in a constant state of change, and our understanding of it is rapidly evolving. Understanding the universe in a naturalistic way doesn't contradict religion, but it does take away some of the original motivations for religion. There are great strides being made in science and this is having an effect on the religious beliefs of individuals. With the rapidly expanding population coupled with the escalating advances in science there will be a need for religions to adapt. The challenge for religions will be to meet the ethical, social and psychological needs of diverse peoples that cannot always be met by governments.

From the earliest humans, mankind has had to adapt to occurrences that were products of nature over which we had no control—ice ages, droughts, floods, global warming, earthquakes, and more. With advancements in science and technology, we now have a greater understanding as to the causes of these environmental conditions. In the future we will have the ability to predict and modify these natural phenomena to better cope with them and perhaps use them to our advantage. Squelching or diverting hurricanes could prevent catastrophic losses such as those encountered from Katrina; diverting precipitation to needed areas could greatly increase crop yields needed to feed a rapidly increasing population.

Advancements in science and technology are necessary to support growth in population, and yet at the same time these advancements are promoting growth in population. On the negative side, people are becoming more dependent on technology and the network of maintenance and support personnel. In the past, catastrophic events were primarily natural disasters and military conflicts. As we become more and more dependent on technology, we are increasingly setting ourselves up for catastrophic events based on technological failures. Many technologies are so complex that it is impossible to adequately anticipate and plan for failure, and attempting to do so is often deemed cost prohibitive. In the future we can expect to see catastrophes relating to technological failures at an increasing rate. Such failures will affect more and more people as the population grows and technological complexities increase.

While evolution is usually for the better, there will always be challenges along the way—challenges for our current generation and future generations to resolve. But, there is hope for a brighter future. In conclusion, here is a poem written by a 9 year old 4th grade student titled *Behind the Gates of Tomorrow*.

> *Behind the gates of tomorrow are children of today*
> *Eating food and dressing in a different manner and way,*
> *Finding new solutions that we could never find*
> *By doing some experiments we never had in mind,*
> *Using new equipment to help the world around*
> *Or making some discoveries that we have never found,*
> *Making better weapons, like guns with magic rays*
> *And with those guns protect our health through lots of weeks and days,*
> *So if you see a person who studies the future way*
> *Say behind the gates of tomorrow are children of today.*

# REFERENCES

Boyle, A. "Tech and Science." *Cosmic Log*. 2011. Web. Daily http://www.msnbc.msn.com.

Cooke, T., ed. *Concise History of World Religions*. Washington, D.C.: *National Geographic,* 2011. Print.

Coyne, G. *The Dance of the Fertile Universe*. 27 Oct 2005. Web. June 2011. www.aei.org/docLib/20051027_HandoutCoynepdf.

Davis, W. K., D. Harrison, & C. H. Howell, eds. *Book of Peoples of the World*. Washington, D.C.: National Geographic, 2007. Print.

Devorkin, D. & R. W. Smith. *Hubble: Imaging Space and Time*. Washington, D.C.: National Geographic, 2008. Print.

Fields, H. "Before There Was Life." *Smithsonian Magazine* Oct 2010: 49. Print

Filippenko, A. "Understanding the Universe." *An Introduction to Astronomy, 2nd Edition*. Chantilly, VA: The Teaching Company, 2008. DVD

Frail, T. A. "Americans Look to 2050." *Smithsonian Magazine 40ᵗʰ Anniversary Special Issue*. July/Aug 2010: 70. Print.

Harrison, K. D. *When Languages Die: The Extinction of the World's Languages and the Erosion of Human Knowledge*. Oxford University Press, 21 July 2008. Print.

Hazen, R. M., & M. Singer. *Why Aren't Black Holes Black*. New York: Doubleday, 1997. Print.

"HubbleSite – Picture Album." *The Universe, Galaxies*. Space Telescope Science Institute's Office of Public Outreach, n.d. Web. Oct 2011
http://hubblesite.org/gallery/album

Kunzig, R. (2011, January). "Population 7 Billion." *National Geographic Magazine* Jan 2011: 32. Print.

Levin, H. L. *Ancient Invertebrates and Their Living Relatives*. New Jersey: Prentice-Hall, Inc, (1999). Print.

MacDonald, G. M. *Biogeography: Space, Time, and Life*. New York: John Wiley & Sons, Inc., 2003. Print.

Mooney, S. "Vendian Period and the Origins of Life." *Paleontology*. 23 Aug. 2011. Web. Oct. 2011.
http://paleontology.edwardtbabinski.us/vendian.html

Panek, R. "The Year of Albert Einstein." *Smithsonian Collectors Edition Magazine* Winter 2011: 40. Print

Prothero, D. R. *Bringing Fossils to Life*. United States: WCB/McGraw-Hill, 1998. Print

Robbins, B. D. "Mythos & Logos" *Blaise Pascal*. 1999. Web. June 2011. http://www.mythosandlogos.com

Seigel, E. "Science Blogs" *Starts with a Bang*. 2011. Web. Daily http://www.scienceblogs.com/startswithabang

Stanley, S. M. *Earth System History*. New York: W. H. Freeman and Company, 1999. Print.

Tarbuck, E. J., & Lutgens, F. K. *Earth: An Introduction to Physical Geology, 5th Edition*. New Jersey: Prentice Hall, 1996. Print.

Than, K. "Live Science" *Hundreds of Human Genes Still Evolving*. 8 Mar 2006. Web. Oct 2011. http://www.live science.com/health/060308_human_evolve.html

The University of Hong Kong. "Astronomers discover complex organic matter exists throughout the universe." *Science Daily*, 26 Oct 2011. Web. 26 Oct 2011. http://www.sciencedaily.com/releases/2011/10/111026 143721.htm

Uthman, E. "Elemental Composition of the Human Body" *Elements of Body*. 7 Feb 2000. Web. Oct 2011. http://web2.airmail.net/uthman/elements_of_body.html.

Whittle, M. "Cosmology" *The History and Nature of Our Universe*. Chantilly, VA: The Teaching Company, 2008. DVD.

Wikipedia – the on-line encyclopedia. *"Blaise Pascal, Pascal's Wager","* Cultures"* Wikipedia, n.d. Web. June 2011. http://www.wikipedia.org.

Zax, D. *"Galileo's Vision."* Smithsonian Collectors Edition Magazine Winter 2011: 12. Print.